The Myths
OF
Creativity

Pamela,

Let's get these ideas
to spread.

Pamela,

Let's get these ideas
to speed.

The Myths

OF

Creativity

THE TRUTH ABOUT HOW INNOVATIVE COMPANIES AND PEOPLE GENERATE GREAT IDEAS

David Burkus

JOSSEY-BASS™

A Wiley Brand

Published by Jossey-Bass
A Wiley Brand
One Montgomery Street, Suite 1200, San Francisco, CA 94104-4594—
www.josseybass.com

Library of Congress Cataloging-in-Publication Data
Burkus, David, date.
   The myths of creativity : the truth about how innovative companies and people generate great ideas / David Burkus. – First edition.
      pages cm
   Includes bibliographical references and index.
   ISBN 978-1-118-61114-2 (hardback);   ISBN 978-1-118-72976-2 (ebk.);
ISBN 978-1-118-72988-5 (ebk.)
   1. Creative ability in business.   2. Creative thinking.   3. New products.   4. Technological innovations.   I. Title.
   HD53.B87 2014
   658.3'14–dc23
                           2013022237

Printed in the United States of America
FIRST EDITION
HB Printing   10 9 8 7 6 5 4 3 2 1

To Janna

Contents

1   The Creative Mythology   1

2   The Eureka Myth   17

3   The Breed Myth   33

4   The Originality Myth   49

5   The Expert Myth   67

6   The Incentive Myth   87

7   The Lone Creator Myth   105

8   The Brainstorming Myth   125

9   The Cohesive Myth   141

10 The Constraints Myth   159

11 The Mousetrap Myth   177

Notes   195

Acknowledgments   203

About the Author   205

Index   207

The Myths

OF

Creativity

The Creative Mythology

There is a mythology that surrounds creativity.

Myths are stories—usually very old stories—that are developed and passed down in an effort to explain why certain mysterious events occur or to affirm how we should behave and think. Cultures develop myths when they can't rely on existing knowledge to explain the world around them. The ancient Greeks told and retold stories of gods, supernatural creatures, and regular mortals as a way to explain how they thought the world worked. The myths they developed were an attempt to explain the mysteries they couldn't readily understand, such as the forces of nature, what happened after death, and even the mysterious process of creativity.

They created the muses, who received and answered the prayers of ancient writers, musicians, and even engineers.[1] The muses were the bearers of creativity's divine spark. They were the source of inspiration. Even thinkers as great as Plato believed that poets drew all of their creativity from the muses, so that any works by the poets were really considered works of the muses.[2] As the Greeks' mythology developed, the muses did as well. Their mythology ultimately included nine muses who acted like patron saints of creativity, each providing mortals with inspired insights in a specific area. Calliope was the muse of epic poetry; Clio, the muse of history; Erato, the muse of love poetry; and so on.

The Greeks believed that all creative insight flowed from these muses, so they worshipped them in search of a creative source and the experience of creating something extraordinary. The act of creating something inspired by the muses was a divine privilege. Some of the greatest minds in Greece at the time, including Plato and Socrates, built shrines for or worshipped at temples dedicated to their muse of choice (or hedged their bets and prayed to them all). The classic Greek epic poems *The Iliad* and *The Odyssey* both open with prayers to a muse.

The Greeks even developed legends to warn against crossing the muses. In one story, Thamyris, a skilled singer, became overly proud of his musical skills. He boasted that he could outsing the muses and challenged them to a contest. The muses indulged his insolence and accepted the challenge. He competed against the muses and lost. The muses did not look kindly on his challenge. They blinded Thamyris and stole his ability to write poetry and play the lyre, leaving him unable to create art ever again. The legend of Thamyris was told to reinforce the belief that gods and the muses were the source of all talent and creative ability. Just as they could bestow it, they could also take it away. The only means of sustaining a creative career, then, was to continue to worship the muses and thank the gods that created them as a means to send their gifts to mortals.

This belief that creativity is a divine gift isn't limited to the ancient Greeks. Theologians from a variety of religions throughout history, including Christianity, asserted that God was the sole source of creativity in the universe.[3] Even into the Middle Ages in Europe, the prevailing belief was that creative ideas were divine and that their derivatives were human. God's blessing was the explanation for all creative talent and inspiration. When one was asked where the idea for a song, poem, or invention came from, the answer of that time was always the same: from God.

Over time, the Greek influence on the Western world ensured that the legend of the muses continued on. It can be seen in literature throughout Western history. In Canto II of Dante's *Inferno*, he cries out to the muses for aid. In *Troilus and Criseyde*, Geoffrey Chaucer woos Clio, asking her to serve as his muse. William Shakespeare's *Henry V* opens with an invocation to the muses in the same style as *The Iliad* and *The Odyssey*. During the Enlightenment, many of the leading thinkers of the eighteenth century sought to reestablish a "cult of the muses" as a means to further their own intellectual pursuits. Voltaire, Danton, and even Benjamin Franklin attended meetings at a Masonic lodge named Les Neufs Soeurs, "the Nine Sisters." Our modern culture still feels the effects of their efforts in such words as *museum*, whose original meaning was "cult place of the muses" but has since come to refer to any place where public knowledge or creative works are displayed.

The remnants of this original mythology appear in many of the conversations I find myself in, such as one I keep having with an old friend of mine from college. We've taken a few writing courses together, and she's always wanted to write a novel. When she came up with the initial concept over ten years ago, she did all the research but never got started on a manuscript. When last we spoke, she was still no closer to writing her novel. She had nothing but a notebook full of research and a blank page. When I ask about her writing, she always gives the same response: "I just couldn't find the inspiration to sit down and write." She may never outwardly say it, but her actions (or lack thereof) reveal a subtle belief that some outside force has to come to her to give her what she needs to write.

Every so often I have a similar conversation with another longtime acquaintance. He has always wanted to start his own business but has so far spent his entire career working inside the same large company. I've lost count of the number of entrepreneurship books he's read or start-up magazines he's purchased. He is always researching, but never creating. He can tell you the specific details of how so many great companies started small and how their growth exploded. "All you need," he tells me, "is a great idea." Just one great idea, and he'd have everything he'd need to become his own boss and start a company that would really make an impact on the world. If only that one idea would come to him from wherever it is waiting in the universe.

While the influence of the Greeks' mythology of creativity can still be seen in modern times, the modern scientific method has helped us move away from a belief in the muses. Research is moving us toward an empirically proven model of creativity that can be used to generate innovative ideas. We don't need to rely on belief in an outside force to generate great ideas. We have everything we need inside ourselves.

If these novel and useful ideas don't come from the divine, then where do they come from? What causes us to be creative in one moment and void in the next? What makes someone more or less creative than his or her peers? Where do our flashes of creative insight come from, and how can we generate more of them? The idea of a sacred being visiting us on occasion to bless us with a creative revelation or that the act of creation should be a near-religious experience might explain why creativity appears so fleeting, but for those who are challenged with being creative on demand, this mythology doesn't really help. Research on creative individuals and innovative organizations does.

Although there is still no precise and agreed-on definition of creativity despite nearly one hundred years of research on the subject, there appears to be at least a small consensus. Creativity is seen by most experts in the field as the process of developing ideas that are both novel and useful.[4] The novel is easily recognized, but the useful is just as important. The Mona Lisa is universally renowned as an important creative work, but a photocopy of the Mona Lisa is probably not considered quite as creative. However, photocopies themselves have been incredibly useful and were also novel when the first office photocopier was released by Xerox in 1959. In organizations, developing ideas, projects, processes, or programs that are both novel and useful is the vital antecedent to leveraging innovation and staying competitive.

There is a unique relationship between creativity and innovation. Teresa Amabile, a Harvard Business School professor, believes that "creativity by individuals and teams is a starting point for innovation" and writes that "the first is a necessary but not sufficient condition for the second."[5] Amabile believes that creativity is the source of innovation, but she does not believe that it comes from the divine. Instead she champions what she calls the "componential model of creativity." Based on decades of research into creativity, this model was designed as a means of explaining the creative process and its various influences.

Amabile's assertion is that creativity is influenced by four separate components: domain-relevant skills, creativity-relevant processes, task motivation, and the surrounding social environment.[6] These four factors determine whether a creative insight will occur. Where they overlap is essentially where creative work happens. The degree to which these factors are present affects the level of creativity an individual will experience. Stated another way, creativity will be strongest when an intrinsically motivated person with significant creative thinking skills and a given level of expertise operates in an environment that supports creativity. Innovation happens when these factors align and the resulting creativity is applied.

Domain-relevant skills (commonly called expertise) are the knowledge, technical skills, or talent an individual possesses in a given domain. These are necessary resources that individuals will utilize as they move through the creative process. Just as it is difficult to imagine a composer writing a symphony without some knowledge of musical keys, scales, and harmony, it is difficult to imagine an architect drafting an office building without knowledge of physics, engineering, building materials, and various other fields of knowledge. In many domains, such as the traditional fine arts, we can easily mistake domain-relevant skills for creativity itself. If we can't imagine being as good as the composer, then we assume that the composer is more creative than us. What we typically don't imagine is the years of deliberate practice required to gain such expertise.

Creativity-relevant processes are the methods people use to approach a given problem and generate solutions. These are the techniques employed to examine a problem from various angles, combine knowledge from various fields, and depart from status quo responses. These skills vary a little depending on personality. Independent risk-takers who can empathize with various perspectives tend to be better creative problem solvers. However, even though a given personality might lend itself to adopting these practices more quickly, the skills can also be learned. Even codependent, risk-averse narcissists can be taught how to generate ideas more easily and combine possible outputs to leverage synergy.

Task motivation is the willingness to engage. Simply put, it is passion. It is the desire to solve a problem for the challenge it poses or the mere satisfaction of working on it. Although expertise and creative thinking are the weapons used to attack creative challenges, no skirmish will be fought until the individual or team agrees to take to the battlefield. The architect with all the right knowledge and the skill to generate new perspectives might be exactly what a client needs, but if she lacks the motivation to engage in the challenge, then those resources will go untapped or be utilized on some other project.

The final influencer, *social environment*, is the only component that exists entirely outside the individual. We all exist inside a larger environment, and that environment influences us more than we're probably aware. Research shows that the environment an individual operates in can either positively or negatively affect creative expression.[7] Are new ideas welcomed or harshly criticized within the organization? Does management emphasize continuous improvement or the status quo? Are there political problems within the organization? Are collaborative, cross-functional teams utilized? Is there freedom in how problems are approached? Are ideas actively shared throughout the organization? All these questions and more must be asked to assess whether the organization's social environment will increase or diminish the creativity of its members.

The elegance of Amabile's model is that it is applicable in a variety of ways. These four factors can be used to adjust the positive or negative influence an organization has on the creativity of its members. If we want our people to generate great ideas, we can analyze our organization according to the four factors. Some of these factors have a wider range of influence than others and thus a more pronounced impact. However, if these four factors are designed with conscious intent, then they will eventually lead to an increase in creative ideas.

Domain skills can be improved. A photographer can learn a new technique for using light, or expand her knowledge into the domain of filmmaking. Likewise a computer programmer can learn more about a specific coding language, learn to code in a new language, or even study a new field like industrial design. Many organizations already utilize the influencer of domain skills through corporate training, job rotation, and even outside learning programs such as tuition reimbursement. However, one requirement of these programs in most companies is that they be specifically relevant to the present job. As we'll examine later, sometimes a broader range of domain knowledge may be a better creativity enhancer than a deeper level of knowledge in the same domain.

Creativity-related processes can be learned. People can learn how to brainstorm (or, more likely, how to brainstorm properly). They can be taught problem-solving methods or lateral thinking techniques. If they can generate more ideas or develop a better ideation process, the quality of their creative work increases. The aforementioned photographer can be shown how to better imagine the staging of portraits or how to combine elements of multiple styles to develop a unique look. The coder can be taught how to design multiple versions of software or how to combine elements of various programs into a new and better offering.

Both expertise and creative methodology can be taught, but their presence is irrelevant without the motivation to work. The photographer may have an inherent understanding of how her lens captures the stories that only she can tell, or she may just sit behind a kiosk and snap portraits for lines of families. The programmer may be working diligently to change the world by designing the next interface between humans and technology, or he may simply be making one more drop-down box to mark the user's country of origin. Fortunately, jobs and programs can be designed to better motivate individuals. In Chapter Six, we'll uncover why designing a job to be intrinsically motivating will yield a better creative return than designing the traditional corporate bonus program.

The social environment of the firm is usually the hardest component to redesign; however, it may also be the most important. The social environment enhances or detracts from creativity by influencing the other three internal components. The level of an organization's commitment to continuous improvement and learning has a direct effect on the ease with which individuals seek to grow their expertise. Likewise, the amount of cross-functional work within the organization affects whether individuals benefit from a broader, group expertise. The openness of top management to new ideas and the availability of resources affect how often creativity-relevant processes are used or how much the "same old, same old" remains the method of choice. Whether top management actively spreads a vision of continuous innovation and reinforces it with actions and policies determines how open individuals are to expressing their creativity. In addition, the emphasis on the impact and significance of the work being done throughout the organization affects how intrinsically motivated individuals are to show up every day and create or innovate.

This four-component model of creativity pulls back the veil on what many believe to be a mysterious and sacred endeavor. Creativity is less the outcome of a divine blessing or visitation and more the result of designing the right ecosystem and filling it with properly trained people with diverse perspectives. While the creative mystics may still pray to the muses or look jealously on the blessed, the implications of this empirically based model are clear: under the right conditions, anyone can be creative. Everyone can generate great ideas.

Despite the empirical challenge Amabile's model provides to a creative mythology, creativity still appears to many as a mysterious process. Even though science has helped explain the original creative mythology, newer myths have developed to help explain away other mysterious elements of creativity and the process of innovation. Perhaps you've had a creative insight, a spark of inspiration, and it felt as though it came from outside yourself. Perhaps you look at another person, and it seems that she was just born with an innate creativity that you lack. Or maybe you look back at our history of progressive invention, and it seems that each idea was a revolutionary and unpredictable departure from the status quo. These things are difficult to explain, so, over time, we've developed a means to explain them. We've developed our own system of heuristics, of speculative formulations, on how creativity works. And these speculations have developed into myths.

One of the possible reasons for the original creative mythology is that new ideas can sometimes seem to appear as a flash of insight. This has also given rise to the *Eureka Myth*, illustrated in stories like the one about Isaac Newton and the falling apple. Instead of a quick spark, however, these insights are actually the result of hard work on a problem or project. The answers are there, but they often need time to incubate in our subconscious as we connect ideas. Sometimes the connection comes from elements of older ideas.

With an ancient, sacred source excluded from the equation, many still view creativity as a limited resource accessible only to a rare breed of individual. This is the *Breed Myth*, the belief that creative ability is a trait inherent in one's personality or genes. We label certain people as "creatives" and others as presumably not. There's little research to support this claim. In fact, the evidence supports the opposite; there is no creative breed. Several companies are structuring their organization to abolish the divide between creative jobs and noncreative ones and make innovation part of everyone's job description.

Often when a creative idea is generated, it becomes immediately viewed as proprietary to the person who thought of it. In business, this is part of the ever-increasing emphasis on intellectual property. This emphasis, however, is based on the *Originality Myth*—that creative ideas are totally original to their creators. The historical record, and empirical research, support a different notion. Ideas are combinations of older ideas, and sharing those ideas helps generate more innovation. This research has some interesting implications for how we treat ideas competitively and even inside an organization.

Most often we rely on a team of experts to generate consistently creative ideas. However, that doesn't always work. Sometimes we get trapped in the *Expert Myth*, the belief that harder problems call for more knowledgeable experts. Instead, research suggests that such wicked problems often require an outsider's perspective. Companies can find ways to tap into these outsiders to find more innovative solutions to difficult problems. Companies that rely on their experts often fall for another myth—the *Incentive Myth*, which argues that incentives, monetary or otherwise, can increase the motivation of their people and hence increase their creative ability. These incentives can help, but often they do more harm than good. Fortunately, nearly fifty years of psychological research into motivation exists to help overcome the incentive-based programs and help design systems that are truly motivating.

When we examine creative work throughout history, certain genius individuals seem to stand out. The *Lone Creator Myth* reflects our tendency to rewrite history to attribute breakthrough inventions and striking creative works to a sole person, ignoring those individuals' influences and collaborations. Creativity is often a team effort, and recent research into creative teams can help leaders build the perfect creative troupe. But often when those teams work, they buy in to the *Brainstorming Myth*, believing that brainstorming alone will yield creative breakthroughs. Unfortunately, though, just "throwing ideas around" is not enough to produce consistently creative breakthroughs.

When we think of exceptionally creative teams working together, we visualize "zany" companies where employees play foosball and joke around while eating free lunches. We think that creative companies must prize safe and cohesive environments built on fun and sharing, but that may not be the case. Believers of this *Cohesive Myth* want everyone to get along and work happily together, when such cohesiveness can actually hinder innovative thinking. Many of the most creative companies have found ways to structure dissent and conflict into their process in order to make sure they produce the best work possible. A similar faulty visualization is given to resources. We think that the companies that produce the most innovative results are those that give their people unlimited resources. This is the *Constraints Myth*—the notion that constraints hinder our creativity. Many companies, however, do just the opposite. They intentionally apply limits to leverage the creative potential of their people because, as research shows, creativity loves constraints.

Many of the myths concern how to be creative, but one myth concerns creativity itself. Many people falsely believe that once we have a creative idea, the work is done. The world will recognize the merit of that idea and help us bring it to life. This is the *Mousetrap Myth*, after the faulty proverb about building a better mousetrap. The world won't beat a path to the door of the most innovative among us. It's more likely that those people and their ideas will be ignored at best, or even actively destroyed and discredited at worst. It's not enough to know how to generate creative ideas; we need to understand how to overcome this phenomenon in order to drive innovation.

Like many traditional myths, the myths of creativity are useful for putting our minds at ease. They seem to explain our world and our creativity (or sometimes our lack thereof). Even if they are not a perfect explanation, embracing the myths is better than shrugging one's shoulders and admitting naïveté. However, as is true of many other myths, embracing them too tightly can hinder our understanding of reality. The myths of creativity might feel helpful, but stubborn belief in them despite evidence to the contrary will hinder us from achieving our creative potential. Once we know the truth, however, we can discard these myths and better prepare ourselves and those we lead to produce real creative thinking. If we want to generate truly great ideas, we can't rely on heuristics or mythology. Instead, we need to closely examine scientific research into the creative mind and study the examples of the most innovative companies and people. We need creativity in organizations, but we need more than just myths of creativity.

Creativity is the starting point for all innovation, and most organizations rely on innovation to create a competitive advantage. Innovation is necessary for the successful development and implementation of new programs or better products. Because of this, leaders of organizations in all industries are asking more questions about creativity. Where does it come from? How can we get more of it? Where do we find creative people? All these questions are valid, but the myths about creativity often lead us to the wrong answers. In order to lead innovation efforts, we must have a better understanding of where creativity comes from and how to enhance the creativity of the people we lead.

We must rewrite the myths.

The Eureka Myth

Although these days we rarely tell stories about the muses visiting mere mortals and inspiring them with creative ideas, the stories we do tell haven't changed all that much. We like stories of epiphanies. We like it when the hero is stuck and suddenly the answer just comes to her. Even if the idea didn't come from a muse, the language we use to retell moments of creative insight still describes these moments as if something arrived from outside the individual. This is the *Eureka Myth*, the notion that all creative ideas arrive in a "eureka" moment. We tell stories about other people's genius ideas as if the idea came suddenly; we conveniently gloss over the tireless concentration that came before the insight, or the hard work of developing the idea that will come afterward. These stories tend to make the idea, not the person, the center of the narrative. I wonder if on some level we like these stories so much because the Eureka Myth offers us another excuse for our own lack of ideas: they just haven't come to us yet. Perhaps one day they will. In the meantime, we cling to well-known stories, like the one about an apple falling from a tree.

We've all heard the story. Isaac Newton sat under an apple tree. The young polymath was contemplating the nature of the universe, stuck on the challenge of explaining what kept it together. As he sat there, back resting against the wide trunk of the apple tree, the tree blessed him with the inspiration he needed. A falling apple struck Newton on the head and triggered something in his mind, causing him to theorize that some force must have been pulling the apple toward the earth. Perhaps the force that pulled the apple might be the same force that pulls upon the moon and keeps it orbiting the earth. Newton had his eureka moment and his answer. The apple fell, and Newton discovered the force of gravity. It's a fascinating and compelling story. Which is why it has stayed around so long despite the event's having never actually happened.

The earliest recorded account of Newton's skirmish with an apple comes from one of his younger contemporaries, William Stukeley, who would eventually write a biography of Newton. In his biography, Stukeley tells the story of how the two shared dinner together at Newton's home and retreated to the garden afterward for tea. Stukeley writes that he and Newton were prompted to discuss gravitation because of the falling of an apple from a tree in the garden. Their discussion ended with the assertion that the size of an object affected its gravitational pull.[1]

That's it. No bombardment of apples. No sudden flash of insight. Stukeley's apple incident could barely be said to have added anything new to what Newton already knew about gravity. At best, the apple encounter Stukeley described could have prompted Newton to begin working on a mathematical formula to explain gravity. But as the story was told and retold by many people, including notable authors such as Voltaire[2] and Isaac Disraeli,[3] the apple gradually changed its trajectory from falling on the grass to falling directly onto Newton.

Next to Newton's apple, the next most popular eureka myth is the story of Archimedes' bath, which actually coined the term *eureka*. Archimedes' cousin, King Hiero, had given Archimedes a special challenge. Hiero had received a crown supposedly made of pure gold. Hiero wanted to know if the gold crown was genuine or fake. Just in case it was genuine, Hiero insisted that Archimedes could not destroy the crown. He could not melt it down or cut into it to examine its composition. After working on the problem for some time, Archimedes decided to relax and take a bath. He filled the tub to the edge and settled in. As he did, he noticed that some of the water had spilled over the side. The presence of his body had caused the water level to rise. Immediately, Archimedes realized he had his solution. He knew that he could determine the density and thus the composition of the crown by submerging it and measuring the displacement of the water. Archimedes was so excited by his revelation that he leaped up from his bath to tell the king. As he ran naked down the streets toward the palace, he reportedly shouted, "Eureka," which in Ancient Greek meant "I've found it!"

Most likely, neither of these stories actually happened as they are now told. But true or not, what these stories ignore is the hard work on either side of the "Eureka." In Newton's case, most of the historical evidence supports that he had already been thinking about gravity's effect on planetary movement. At best, the fall of the apple only triggered Newton's mind into making the connection between the pull of gravity on small, planet-shaped objects (like apples) and the possibility that a large pull existed between the earth and the moon. Even after the apple incident, it was several years before Newton presented a finalized mathematical explanation for gravity. Likewise, in the case of Archimedes, we tend to ignore the work he'd done before relaxing to take a bath. Somehow Archimedes must have learned or calculated the formulas for how to turn a water displacement measurement into a measurement of density. After the bath, of course, he actually had to take the measurements and run the calculations.

These two accounts are the most famous, but certainly not the only stories involving the Eureka Myth. When stories of creative insight or sudden inspiration are told, many elements seem to get left behind in the retelling. In the case of Newton, his own retelling of the story may have pruned away some of the more accurate details. These are definitely more entertaining renditions of these stories, but they are far less truthful. The Eureka Myth doesn't offer much in the way of guidance for generating creative ideas or innovative breakthroughs. Instead, the myth reduces idea generation into something more providential—if you're in the right place at the right time, then your idea will manifest itself when triggered by something outside your control. There's nothing in the Eureka Myth, nothing in these stories, to tell us how to produce these moments of insight. If something sudden does happen, what inside the mind triggers it? Surely there has to be something we can do to help trigger a creative revelation besides being hit by falling apples or spilling water onto our bathroom floor.

Psychologist Mihaly Csikszentmihalyi has been searching for that something. In one of his more famous research projects, he studied the thought processes of ninety-one prominent creative individuals, including writer Robertson Davies and famed scientists Linus Pauling and Jonas Salk. Rather than probing the inner workings of their minds through psychological testing or brain imaging, Csikszentmihalyi focused his research on their own perspectives of the thought process they each used. His goal was to understand how they believed they generated their creative insight. In short, he was looking for how they produced eureka moments, if they produced them at all. What he found was that almost all of the people he studied shared a similar creative process that consisted of five stages: preparation, incubation, insight, evaluation, and elaboration.[4] Note that Csikszentmihalyi's stages include a moment of insight, when it feels as though all the pieces of the puzzle have fallen into assembly. However, where the Eureka Myth would tell us that these insights are triggered by a chance happening, Csikszentmihalyi has placed this moment in the center of a larger and more elaborate process. It includes one stage that is often overlooked, especially inside our working life: incubation.

Incubation is the stage where people briefly step back from their work. Many creative people intentionally set a project aside and take a physical break from their work, believing that this incubation stage is where knowledge from preparation is digested and ideas begin to come together below the threshold of the conscious mind. Some people juggle various projects at the same time under the belief that while their conscious mind is focusing on one project, the others are incubating in the unconscious. In fact, these incidents are more common than the famed eureka moments of Newton and Archimedes. Edison, Michelangelo, Darwin, van Gogh, and da Vinci all took on various different projects simultaneously, regularly switching back and forth between them.[5] Csikszentmihalyi's research allows for this, asserting that the unconscious mind is capable of keeping many ideas incubating in parallel, even if the conscious mind can focus on only one thing at a time. He writes that "cognitive accounts of what happens during incubation assume . . . that some kind of information processing keeps going on even when we are not aware of it, even while we are asleep."[6] Once the incubation stage has run its course, which could be a few days or several years, it should lead a person into the insight stage. This is where the feeling of "eureka" happens, where the ideas being incubated have fermented into a possible solution that can be tested and implemented. Sometimes the insight can seem as though it came from nowhere; other times it still takes intense focus on the project to yield a productive insight.

Csikszentmihalyi wasn't the first to describe such a series of stages. Late in the nineteenth century, French mathematician Henri Poncairé attempted to describe the process of creative discovery in four distinct phases: preparation, incubation, illumination, and verification. Poncairé's four stages are quite similar to the five stages Csikszentmihalyi's creative geniuses described. Although both describe the moment of illumination and the requirement of verification, the period of incubation is perhaps the most aligned. Both Poncairé and Csikszentmihalyi argued that eureka moments don't just happen; they are preceded by research and preparation and are birthed from a period of mental unfocus.

If Poncairé and Csikszentmihalyi's concept of incubation is accurate, then it should be possible to prove the occurrence of incubation empirically. It turns out that it is possible, but quite difficult—so difficult, in fact, that researchers have only recently found evidence for an incubation effect. A team of psychology researchers from the Centre of the Mind at the University of Sydney designed an experiment that divided ninety undergraduate psychology students into three groups.[7] Each group was tasked with completing what is known as an *alternate uses test*, in which participants list as many possible uses for common objects as they can imagine. In this case, the participants were told to list possible uses for a piece of paper. The number of original uses that were generated would serve as a measurement of divergent thinking, an important element of creativity. The first group worked on the problem for four continuous minutes. The second group was interrupted after two minutes and tasked with generating synonyms for each word from a given list (considered to be another task that required creativity), then given two more minutes to complete the original test. The final group was interrupted after two minutes and given the Myers-Briggs Type Indicator (considered a completely unrelated task), then given two more minutes to continue working on the original alternate uses test. But all groups were given a total of four minutes to work on their list of possible uses for a sheet of paper. The research team was then able to compare the creativity that resulted from continuous work, work with an incubation period during which a related task was completed, and work with an incubation period during which an unrelated task was completed. The researchers found that the group given a break to work on an unrelated task (the Myers-Briggs test) generated the most ideas, averaging 9.8 ideas in four minutes. The group given a break to work on a related task placed second, averaging 7.6 ideas generated. The group given no break but four continuous minutes of work time generated the fewest possible uses, averaging 6.9 ideas. The research team had validated the idea that incubation periods, even those as brief as a few minutes, can significantly boost a person's creative output.

Another study, this one led by Benjamin Baird, a psychologist at the University of California, Santa Barbara, whose research focuses on the role of conscious attention in thought processes, offers a peek inside the minds of the incubating participants in the aforementioned study.[8] The participants in Baird's study went through a series of tests similar to those of the previously described subjects, except that instead of doing related or unrelated tasks as incubation time, they were given tasks that were cognitively demanding or undemanding. Demanding tasks required working memory and cognitive processing; undemanding tasks simply required reaction time. A control group worked only on creative problems, with no break task. After their incubation task, the participants were given a commonly used survey that measured the frequency that participants' minds wandered during the task, such as when thinking about personal worries, past events, or future plans. Not surprisingly, participants performing the undemanding incubation task reported that their minds had wandered significantly more than those performing the demanding task. Those whose minds had wandered most also scored significantly better on their creative measures—they reported more possible uses for their objects. Baird and his team showed that incubation periods which allow the mind to wander offer a significantly stronger boost to creativity, suggesting that individuals whose minds regularly wander may be more creative in general. Such mind-wanderers appear to have tapped into the power of incubation.

There are a lot of different explanations for why incubation works to produce eureka moments or creativity boosts. Besides giving your mind the chance to rest, one of the more popular explanations is known as "selective forgetting." When presented with complicated problems, the mind can often get stuck, finding itself tracing back through certain pathways of thinking again and again. When you work on a problem continuously, you can become fixated on previous solutions. You will just keep thinking of the same uses for that piece of paper instead of finding new possibilities. Taking a break from the problem and focusing on something else entirely gives the mind some time to release its fixation on the same solutions and let the old pathways fade from memory. Then, when you return to the original problem, your mind is more open to new possibilities. When this return is triggered by a chance event or observation, it can often feel like the eureka moment of the Newton and Archimedes legends.

It's likely that Newton found the beginnings of his formula for gravity and Archimedes realized his method for testing the golden crown after a period of incubation. They allowed their minds to relax, and a chance observation directed their attention back to their problems, causing them to stumble on new possibilities. It was incubation that led to a solution, not falling apples or spilled bathwater. So why do the eureka stories persist? Probably because history has a story-centric nature, and tales of fallen apples and relaxing baths are far more engaging than the truth.

In the 1930s, Norman Maier designed an experiment to explain why we describe our moments of insight as sudden inspiration.[9] Maier was a renowned experimental psychologist who did most of his work at the University of Michigan. In his experiment on moments of insight, he set individual participants in a large room filled with an assortment of objects, from extension cords and poles to tables and chairs. From the ceiling, Maier had suspended two long ropes, one in the center of the room and one next to the wall. Although the ropes were long, they were placed far enough away from each other that you couldn't grasp one rope and walk over to the other. Maier's challenge to each participant was simple: tie the two ropes together. Specifically, think of as many methods as possible to connect the ropes.

There are a variety of solutions to Maier's problem, and the majority of participants came up with three fairly easily. Most participants thought (1) to move one rope as close as it could get, tie it to a piece of furniture, and then grab the second rope and bring it to the tied-down rope; (2) to tie the extension cord to the end of one rope and pull it to the other; and (3) to use a pole to fish one rope and drag it to the other. While most participants thought of these three solutions, a minority thought of a fourth: set the first rope swinging back and forth, then grab the second rope and walk toward the swinging rope, catching it when it swung close enough to be reached. For those in the majority, who didn't think of this solution on their own, Maier gave them a small hint. Ten minutes into the experiment, he walked by one rope and "accidentally" brushed it with just enough force to start it swinging. After watching this subtle motion, most of the participants thought of the fourth solution. Strangely, when Maier later asked all the participants how they thought of the swinging solution, only one mentioned Maier's accidental brush. The rest described it as a flash of insight and constructed elaborate explanations of their thought processes involving things like monkeys swinging from trees or childhood tire swings. Maier's experiment demonstrates what most psychologists call *confabulation*—in hindsight, people are often quick to invent explanations for unknown behaviors. Confabulation is how stories of falling apples are written. When incubation yields insight from an unknown source, confabulation is there to help develop a grander and more satisfying tale.

Although an empirical explanation of the Eureka Myth is vital to understanding the truth about innovation, it's equally important to emphasize that neither Newton nor Archimedes would have ever had his eureka moment without going through the other stages in Csikszentmihalyi's creative thought process. Without adequate preparation, their minds may never have generated the correct solution. Likewise, without evaluation and elaboration, their ideas would not have been validated, and we might still be without a formula for gravity. In addition, without the incubation process and the elaboration that follows, we might also be without another life-changing innovation: the Post-it Note.

In 1966, a young chemist named Spencer Silver joined the R&D division of 3M (Minnesota Mining and Manufacturing Company). After two years of working on various projects, Silver turned his attention to improving one of the company's more established product lines: adhesives. Silver worked on this project off and on for five years but was only able to develop an inferior adhesive.[10] Whenever he tinkered with the formula, he could only produce an adhesive that was less sticky than existing products. He felt that there had to be a use for what he was working on, but was unable to figure out what that was. Silver persisted, showing the project to as many people in the company as he could, hoping they might be able to find a use for his technology. Unfortunately for Silver, it seemed as though no one he talked to could help him.

Art Fry, a chemical engineer to whom Silver had once presented the project, was a singer in his church's choir. Fry struggled with how to mark the pages in his hymnal without damaging the book. Bookmarks worked, but they had a tendency to fall out when he opened the book while he was singing. One Sunday morning when Fry was in church, his mind drifted to the stalled project, and he connected the dots

28

between his hymnal and Silver's project. If he were to coat his bookmarks with Silver's glue, they would stay inside his hymnal to mark the pages during the service but could later be removed without damaging the book. Fry returned to work, contacted Silver, and for two years the duo worked on a prototype for a semipermanent bookmark as an unauthorized side project, eventually building a manufacturing setup in the basement of Silver's home. After several more years tinkering with manufacturing, they presented the product to people inside 3M. The reaction was positive; people enjoyed using the removable bookmark, and word quickly spread. But there was a problem. Most of the test bookmarks were used once. They were tucked inside a book, and the book was placed on a shelf to wait for the reader's return. If the bookmarks were reused, Fry's colleagues would just remove them from one book and put them in another. The product worked well, but it wasn't being used often enough to show market demand.

A few weeks later, while working on an unrelated project, Fry had another insight. He was reviewing a report and was unclear about a particular paragraph. Instead of writing a memo or making a phone call, Fry reached for one of his removable bookmarks. He wrote his question on the bookmark and stuck it to the report before sending the document up to his supervisor. To his surprise, his supervisor returned the report with the answer to Fry's question written on a different bookmark and stuck on top of Fry's original. Fry realized that these bookmarks could be used as a way to communicate. He could leave brief notes to colleagues and stick them in places where they would be easily seen. "During a coffee break we thought, 'Aha! we don't have just a bookmark, what we have is a whole systems approach,'" Fry said, recounting his and Silver's second discovery.[11] Fry distributed the bookmarks throughout his company with new instructions: to write notes on them. Within a few weeks, the offices of 3M were filled with small squares of paper stuck to every imaginable surface.

In 1980, a full twelve years after Silver's invention of an "inferior adhesive," 3M released the Post-it Note to the mass market. On the surface, this story looks like another tale of eureka moments. But consider the story against Csikszentmihalyi's five-stage creative thought process. Silver and Fry spent whatever time they could in the preparation stage. They would experiment with the formula, tinker with a manufacturing process, and even discuss the project with various colleagues. Because it was a side project, they were forced to constantly take incubation periods to refocus on their main projects. It was during one of these incubation periods that Fry had his first insight, sticking the adhesive onto bits of paper and using them as bookmarks. Silver and Fry moved from this insight into evaluation, but the evaluation wasn't great. It was a good product, but not one with much market potential. Again during another incubation period, Fry had his second insight: he used the bookmark as a note. This time, when they moved to evaluation and elaboration, they found success. Even after both insights, there was still much work that needed to be done to test whether the eureka moments' insights had helped them create a marketable product.

We like stories of sudden inspiration like that of Newton and the apple or Archimedes and the bathtub. However, just as in the case of the Post-it Note, these flashes of genius are actually part of a larger process of creative work. Each stage in the process is vital to innovation. Without preparation, our mind doesn't have much material to work with. Without incubation, we can become fixated on solutions that don't work and never generate the insight we need. Even after we have an insight, we must evaluate our idea and elaborate on it before it becomes something tangible. The Eureka Myth can lead people astray, encouraging them to sit underneath trees or take endless baths hoping for the right moment of inspiration. The lesson of incubation is to work hard on a creative task or difficult problem, but to shift tasks when we get stuck, giving ourselves permission to let our minds wander to something else for a little while. We might just find that our mind drifts back to the problem, but this time it offers a new solution.

The Breed Myth

Although creativity isn't a gift from the muses or something that comes exclusively to a small group of individuals in a spectacular insight, it can still seem as though creative individuals are a select group. It feels as if the people we view as outstandingly creative are just a certain breed—that they are cut from different cloth than the rest of us. Sometimes they even appear different on the surface. Because they look and act so different, we're tempted to assume that they must be different underneath. This is what I call the *Breed Myth*, the notion that creative individuals are a different breed from normal humans or that something in their genetic code draws them to more creative pursuits. We're eager to believe that some people are born creative and others drew a different genetic hand. When we look at outstandingly creative individuals in the arts or design fields, they don't seem to conform to the business-as-usual types. If we believe that they are different or that they have something we don't, then we have a safe rationalization for believing that we're not as innovative as they are. If we don't share their creative genes, then we can rest in that comfortable excuse every time we're called on to generate new ideas. "I'm just not creative," we can say, and shirk the responsibility to think innovatively.

In many organizations, there is even a clear distinction between "creative" types and "suits." The "suits" occupy the traditional business disciplines, accounting, finance, operations, and management. The "creatives" can be found in different departments: marketing, advertising, or design. They are easy to spot; they rarely wear suits. In many organizations, these departments are kept separate from each other, and sometimes the rules even apply differently to one group than to another. In the United States, the distinction has made its way into how companies process payroll. The current U.S. tax code allows organizations certain exemptions from federal minimum wage and overtime regulations if the nature of the exempted individual's work meets its definition of "creative."[1] The U.S. Department of Labor actually makes a distinction between traditional professions and creative professions. Traditional professions involve work that depends on "intelligence, diligence, and accuracy," whereas creative professions involve "invention, imagination, originality, or talent." If even the IRS has spoken on the matter, then clearly the chasm between creatives and suits is wide and entrenched.

The distinction goes beyond individuals in organizations. Often we separate whole businesses into various categories, making a point to label which businesses fall into the "creative

34

industries." Although these distinctions are made mostly for the purposes of analyzing the economy of a region or country, they still demonstrate the belief that certain occupations are filled with people who are creative, and presumably others house their noncreative counterparts. It's easy to look at the output from design firms and entertainment companies and find creativity. It's a lot harder to recognize the creativity in a place like Walmart, despite its drastic innovations in areas like product pricing and supply chain management.

This distinction explains why the Breed Myth is persistent. Because we have that separation, we also want a simple, preferably biological reason for why some people seem incredibly creative and others do not. Perhaps the most telling anecdote has to do with Albert Einstein's brain. After Einstein's death, his brain was removed and preserved (despite his request that his body be cremated).[2] Psychologists and medical doctors alike subjected the brain to close examination in hopes of finding a biological explanation for his creativity and genius. In the case of Einstein, none of the studies revealed any significant difference between his brain and the brain of most humans—except for the surprising find that his brain was significantly *smaller* in mass than the average male brain. This wasn't exactly what they had hoped to find, so their search continues.

Over a half a century ago, in 1950, Dr. J. P. Guilford inspired a generation of researchers by challenging them to prove where creativity came from and whether creatives really were a breed of their own. He had just been elected president of the American Psychological Association (APA), and as the newly minted leader of psychology's premiere gathering of research scientists, he was scheduled to give the keynote at their annual meeting—his first presidential address.[3] Traditionally, the presidential address is intended to be a time for APA presidents to call attention to a prominent issue that they believe requires greater psychological research. Guilford had spent much of his life researching psychology, and during his career, he developed a massive program of psychological testing for the U.S. military. On this day, he stood before the assembled crowds to announce that he believed that the next area of focus for the APA should be creativity.

At the time, little psychological research on creative individuals or the creative process had been done, and most people held unproven stereotypes about creative people. Creatives were often envisioned as long-haired neurotics who retreated from society to a lonely studio or cabin in the wilderness to focus on their craft. Guilford's message questioned the accuracy of these stereotypes. The research he called for was meant to prove just how poorly most preconceptions of creative individuals reflected reality, encouraging the development of a means to psychologically explain the creative process. Decades after Guilford's address, however, the lingering influence of these stereotypes can still be felt.

If there is a creative type, a particular breed of human specifically designed for creative pursuits, then we should be able to discover it by examining two particular areas: personality and genetics. Some people have personalities that enable them to see connections between seemingly unconnected concepts or that make them more willing to risk the judgment that comes with creating. It may well be that the particular personality traits that make a person creative will be represented in their genetic code. Fortunately for our purposes, creativity researchers, as well as psychologists and geneticists, have been examining just those assumptions.

Shortly after Guilford's seminal address, research on the shared personality traits of creative individuals began. The most prominent of this early research came from the Institute for Personality Assessment and Research (IPAR) at the University of California, Berkeley.[4] IPAR began by having a pool of experts nominate the most creative people in their field. The nominated creatives were invited to spend the weekend in Berkeley to participate in the study. While much of the weekend consisted of shared meals and informal discussions, IPAR researchers also subjected their nominees to a variety of testing and found that many of them shared similar traits, including above-average intelligence, openness to new experiences, balanced personalities, and a preference for complexity. Although these traits helped differentiate this particular group of people from the population as a whole, they failed to establish what differentiated creative people from their noncreative counterparts. The list generated by IPAR revealed shared traits, but they were hardly uniform, and there was no comparison to a general population. There was no way of knowing from the institute's research what made creative people different from normal individuals, or even if they were all that different. Future studies would provide such comparisons.

As the field of personality research progressed, eventually a standard system of measurements was developed that made it possible to easily draw comparisons between two groups of individuals. The most commonly used measurement is the five-factor model of personality (also called the "Big Five"). The five-factor model was first discovered in the 1960s, but wasn't readily adopted until the 1980s. The Big Five measures an individual on five personality scales: openness to experience, conscientiousness, extraversion, agreeableness, and neuroticism. Instead of classifying individuals into certain types, like the DISC or Meyers-Briggs tests used so often by organizations, the Big Five test reveals an individual's personality as numerical scores on the five personality scales. Instead of placing individuals inside one of a fixed set of categories, it is a system for describing the subtle differences among individuals' personalities. In their quest to uncover a creative personality, researchers eventually adopted the Big Five as a way to compare the personality measurements of creative standouts to those of a general population (presumably non-creative). If creative people all tended to score higher than average in some of the dimensions, then we could begin to see the template for a creative personality. However, the evidence for a creative personality is mixed at best. While openness to experience shows the strongest correlation to creativity, there is little solid evidence linking creativity to any of the others.[5] These results imply that creativity isn't the exclusive domain of one kind of personality. There isn't one particular creative personality type.

With personality out of the picture, it makes sense to look to genetics for some validation of the Breed Myth. Since the discovery of genes and the mapping of our genetic code, scientists have continued to hunt for genetic explanations for much of human behavior. We're eager to attribute human behaviors to some innate biological source, and genetics have promising potential to do so. We're fascinated with the idea that nature might let nurture off the hook. We've been searching for a music gene, an obesity gene, and yes, even a creativity gene. Such biological explanations are hard to argue with. And if creativity is determined by our genes, then once we find out that we are or are not coded to be creative, we can start down the right career path. If creativity is decided at birth, then organizations that want to enhance their creativity just need to identify those who have won the creative birth lottery.

If you want to study the influence of genetics on creativity or music or any other trait, then you have to start with families.[6] This is difficult, though, because not every family will do. In a typical family, children experience the same parenting styles, and their genes come from the same pool. They share the same home but only half the genes of their siblings. In such an arrangement, the influence of genetics and the influence of upbringing are too closely woven together. In these families, it is too difficult to sort out what can be attributed to nature and what can be attributed to nurture. However, there is a special kind of family that allows such distinctions to be made: families with twins.

On the surface, families with twins appear to pose the same research challenge as regular families—they weave biology and upbringing too closely together. However, because there are both identical (or monozygotic) twins, who share the exact same genetic code, and fraternal (or dizygotic) twins, who only share half their genes, it's possible to examine large samples of identical and fraternal twins and make educated claims about what traits come from genetics and what traits come from experience. We can compare nature and nurture. If identical twins are more similar than fraternal twins, then the cause is likely nature. If there isn't a noticeable difference between the two groups' similarity, then the cause is likely nurture. To conduct a study of creativity and genetics, you need to find a large sample of both kinds of twins.

In 1973, a team of researchers led by psychologist Marvin Reznikoff set out to do just that. They tapped the Connecticut Twin Registry, which maintains a listing of all multiple births that occurred in the state of Connecticut since 1897, and conducted a comprehensive study of creativity among twins.[7] From the registry list, Reznikoff's team put together a group of 117 twins and divided them by gender and by zygosity (whether the twins were identical or fraternal). The participants were given a battery of eleven different tests designed to gauge their creative abilities. Each test measured a different element of what contributes to creative ability, such as the ability to generate large quantities of ideas or to apply existing concepts in new ways. This method would allow the researchers to calculate the measurements of creativity and see if there were significant differences in the rates of similarity between identical or fraternal twins. When they tabulated the results, they found almost no significant distinctions. In their published paper, they write, "There is little consistent or compelling evidence, however, to support the notion of a genetic component in creativity."[8] Where the research team did find similarities between twins, their rates were no better than similarities randomly distributed throughout the general population. This evidence implies that the twin similarities result from their environment and not their genetic code. They found no evidence for a creativity gene. Nature couldn't explain away nurture.

If creativity isn't limited to specific types and creative ability is not a result of the genetic lottery, then why does the strict separation in some organizations continue? Why do we insist on segregation between creative and noncreative roles? If creativity is within the grasp of every person, in every department or industry, then perhaps the way we structure our organizations should reflect that integration and make it possible for everyone to contribute his or her own creativity. There are a few companies out there that have done just that, and they've found that the integration enhances their innovation and profitability.

At W. L. Gore & Associates, all employees start in the same position: associate.[9] There is no clearly defined assignment and no ladder to climb if the assignment is completed well. Instead, new associates are paired with a "sponsor"—a longtime associate who helps translate the company jargon, introduces new hires to the larger organization, and guides them through the first few weeks of rotating around on different project teams. This is the life of new associates for several months, meeting people and learning about projects. It's an audition phase, designed to find the right fit between a new associate's skills and desires and the needs of a particular project team. And there are a lot of project teams.

Gore was founded in 1958 by Wilbert "Bill" L. Gore as an alternative to the large, bureaucratic organizations most people were used to. Bill Gore had just left a seventeen-year career at DuPont, where he believed the market potential of polytetra-fluoroethylene (PTFE, or Teflon) was being significantly underestimated. Gore had spent some time inside smaller, entrepreneurial-feeling R&D teams while at DuPont, and he hoped to find a way to ensure that his new company had a similar feel. He wanted all his employees to feel free to invest their time in projects they felt passionate about or to invent their own projects. To accomplish this, he created a structure at W. L. Gore & Associates that was drastically different from the large conglomerate bureaucracies common at the time.

In 2010, W. L. Gore and its more than eight thousand associates generated nearly $3 billion in revenue from a diverse set of products. Their most well-known product, Gore-Tex, is made from the very PTFE technology that Bill Gore left to experiment with. His son, Robert, discovered how to stretch the material into a threadlike polymer that was durable and porous, and that discovery became a platform for hundreds of products from boots and gloves to medical products to the space suits worn by NASA astronauts. Gore even used PTFE technology to create a stronger, less breakable dental floss. Gore sold the technology, now called Oral-B Glide, to Procter & Gamble in 2003, but continues to manufacture and develop the product.

Although W. L. Gore's products are certainly innovative, its unique structure is the company's true innovation. Gore has a formal CEO and is organized into four major divisions:

fabrics, electronics, medical, and industrial. Beyond those elements, however, the entire organization looks quite flat. Instead of a hierarchy, Gore is structured as what it calls a lattice. This lattice is a horizontal structure in which everyone is connected to everyone else. The lines of communication are direct, and the responsibilities are lateral. There are no real organizational charts, no ladders to climb, and no departmental distinctions between creative and noncreative roles. Gore's core structural units are the self-managed teams of associates who band together around each project. These associates are responsible to each other. They rely on each other's creative contribution to a project's success, and they even determine each other's compensation.

Without a series of management tiers, there is no formalized system for green-lighting projects. So Gore relies on its lattice to develop new products. When someone has a new idea, he or she starts working to develop it and asks for help as needed. As people join the project, it gains momentum. If no one joins, the project suffocates. Although there are no formal titles at Gore—nothing distinguishes the PhD scientist from the marketing expert or the operations manager—there is one title that associates can have added to their business card: leader. A leader is someone who has started several projects or is asked to serve as a project leader often. Even their CEO (which their corporate charter requires) is selected via a collaborative process between the board of directors and a cross-section of Gore associates.

Before Dave Myers became a leader, Gore wasn't in the guitar string business. Myers, an engineer by training, was working on a cardiac implant project at a Gore plant in Flag-staff, Arizona, when he started experimenting with ways to improve his mountain bike cables by coating them with the same polymer used to make Gore-Tex fabric. After Myers made a successful prototype (and likely a great mountain bike ride), his mind wandered from his mountain bike to his guitar. Myers knew that guitar strings lose their tonal integrity as skin oils build up around and inside the steel coils. So he assembled a team of volunteer associates, and together they began to experiment with coating guitar strings with the Gore-Tex polymer. After three years of off-and-on experiments, the team created a guitar string that held its tone longer than any other string in the industry. It was an immediate hit in the market, and Elixir guitar strings still continue to outsell all other U.S. competitors.

Although W. L. Gore's four divisions do provide some degree of structure, it is common for people to work on projects across those four divisions. To facilitate collaboration, Gore intentionally keeps its plants small, usually fewer than two hundred people, and generally builds plants in clusters around each other. This allows everyone working in one plant to become familiar with one another, but also allows potential project leaders to move beyond their plant to others in the cluster when they need help—just as Myers did with his guitar string project. In this way, individuals from all backgrounds can join forces around a new creative project.

In a traditional organization, it's hard to imagine an engineer working on a medical device while simultaneously experimenting with mountain bike cables and guitar strings. But W. L. Gore is no traditional company. Its unique structure means that its employees don't spend time worrying about traditional labels or whether a project is in their department. There are no preconceptions about who is or isn't creative. Instead, if associates are interested and feel that they can contribute to a project, even one as new to the company as guitar strings, they make a commitment to the project and start contributing. Because there isn't a certain department for developing ideas or even a separation between product development ideas and marketing ideas, the entire Gore organization is a creative marketplace where people invest their time in the projects that appeal to them, and sometimes even compete for the ability to work on a new and promising project. This breeding ground for ideas is what allowed the company to grow to a portfolio of over one thousand different products, from the fabric in space suits to the strings on a guitar.

Gore is a unique organization with truly innovative products. In fact, its uniqueness makes it easy to dismiss as an outlier. The company was built from the start around the lattice idea and around the mission of developing new and innovative products. Perhaps Gore can avoid the traditional distinctions because it has been that way since its inception, but what about "normal" companies? Can such an idea be implemented in a traditional organization? It turns out that it already has.

In 1980, industrialist Antonio Curt Semler passed the ownership of his manufacturing company, Semco, to his son Ricardo.[10] The company was founded three decades earlier, shortly after the senior Semler had immigrated from Vienna, Austria, to settle in São Paulo, Brazil. Over time, Antonio built

Semco from a one-man operation in his small apartment to a company with $4 million in revenue and a hundred employees. He did it by following the traditional rules of industrial management. As he grew, he built a hierarchical structure in which management wrote policies and procedures, creating binders of specifications for every possible circumstance. Although this method worked at first to grow the company, that growth had slowed and eventually began to reverse by the time Ricardo took over.

The company Ricardo inherited was on the verge of bankruptcy. The traditional hierarchy wasn't performing well, and Ricardo needed a drastic shift. He needed innovation. He needed creativity, and he needed it from every level—from factory workers *and* from senior managers. The junior Semler decided to restructure the organization in hopes of allowing innovative ideas to develop at any level. Semler knew that not everyone would allow that to happen, so on his first day, he fired 60 percent of his top-level management team. At first, he attempted to restructure Semco as a matrixed organization, in which individuals were assigned to different projects, sometimes in different departments on an as-needed basis. When this failed to achieve the turnaround, Semler ditched the concept of assignments all together. He created a fluid organization in which teams formed and reformed around ideas and projects, and individuals self-selected in and out of those projects as desired. Although this might seem like a chaotic lack of structure, at Semco, individuals determine the structure by their actions. "That's not a lack of structure," Semler argues, "that's just a lack of structure imposed from above."[11] Management doesn't make the distinction between creatives and suits; individuals decide for themselves what skills they have and where they can be useful.

Because Semler built an organization where individuals make the decisions about how to use their creativity, they use it more often. Eventually, Semler pulled back even further from making decisions, not just about people but about everything. In 2003, Semco threw a celebration to mark the tenth anniversary of the last decision the CEO made. The lack of top-down decision making and the democratization of innovation appear to be paying off. Also in 2003, Semco celebrated annual revenues of $212 million, a substantial turnaround for a company that was once nearly bankrupt.

W. L. Gore and Semco are illustrations of how continuous innovation can flourish in an organization that accepts the creative potential of all its members. The Breed Myth doesn't survive in places like Gore or Semco, where everyone can propose ideas and find himself or herself leading a team. Instead of imposing departmental separation between creative and noncreative types, Semco created an organizational structure in which the projects and products, not an assumed genetic distinction or a self-imposed differentiation, affect one's role. Instead of managers using the creatives-and-suits distinction to draw up a top-down hierarchy, Gore lets its people self-select into roles where they can use the creative insights they have, even in ways the U.S. Department of Labor might not classify as "creative."

It's easy to trust the Breed Myth. It's easy to believe that some are born creative and others less so. Our current understanding of genetics leaves us eager to explain away creative ability as coded into someone's genes and thus downplay the creative potential of others. Even the bureaucratic rules surrounding labor and human resources rely on the Breed Myth, specifying a supposed distinction between positions that demonstrate creativity and those that do not. But the evidence supports a different conclusion. Creative ability isn't limited to a particular personality type, and it isn't controlled by our genetic code. When traditional organizations separate those they think are creative from those they think are not, they are severely limiting their own potential for success. Smart organizations, like W. L. Gore and Semco, have abandoned this false division altogether and have structured themselves so that creativity arises from across the entire firm. Every organization wanting to stay competitive in an innovation-driven economy needs creativity from every one of its people. We need innovative ideas too much to seek them out from only those of a certain, imaginary breed.

The Originality Myth

Ideas, we assume, are generated in the mind of one individual and brought to life by that same individual's effort. When we tell stories about a new invention, we assume that its creator is entirely responsible for dreaming up the device as a complete whole. We like to believe that each new idea is as unique as its creator's brain, fingerprint, or genetic code, and have a tendency to remember a creative idea or innovation as the product of one person or one company. We want our ideas to be seen as unique and wholly original; therefore, others' ideas must also have been as unique. This is the *Originality Myth*— the faulty belief that we would not have a given creation without its single creator and that the creator's idea is wholly original. The Originality Myth lets us assume total credit for a new idea and claim that idea as our property or the property of our organization. Yet new ideas don't occur so simply. Rather, a close examination of history reveals a different perspective on creativity. Ideas develop through a much more complicated path, often involving more than just one person. In our quest to recognize sole geniuses, we sometimes edit the history of a creative idea until we're left with just one creator. Consider one of the well-known stories we tell of a single creator and his innovative new creation: the telephone.

In 1874, Alexander Graham Bell was taking a break from his normal life in Boston, which involved working as a speech therapist while struggling to find a means of creating what he called the "harmonic telegraph."[1] One evening, he took a walk to a bluff that overlooked the Grand River near his parents' house in Bratford, Ontario. Bell stumbled upon a secluded spot on the bluff created by a fallen tree. In this spot, he found the time and freedom to let his mind wander, and he ultimately came up with the solution to his problem: a way to convey sound using electric currents instead of sound waves. When he returned to Boston, he began to work furiously on a prototype of his imagined device. Bell converted his attic into a personal laboratory and hired Thomas Watson as a research assistant. When the prototype was in working order, it was Watson on the receiving end of Bell's device. On February 14, 1876, Bell filed notice with the U.S. Patent Office in Washington, DC.[2]

The telephone was born. Twice.

That same day, another notice was filed at that same patent office. Elisha Gray, himself an accomplished inventor, filed a patent caveat for a remarkably similar device.[3] Gray had a significant history of working with telegraph technology. He had invented the self-adjusting relay switch and the telegraph printer—both of which had moved the telegraph industry forward drastically. He had set his sights on the transmission of sound through the telegraph around the same time as Bell and, coincidently, filed his invention with the U.S. Patent Office on the same day in the same location.

After both patents were registered, Bell began work making telephones and founded the company that would eventually become AT&T. Gray went into partnership with Thomas Edison and made telephones for Western Union, with which he'd worked closely for many years—until Bell sued Gray. Gray, who many believe developed a better telephone, settled the lawsuit and abandoned his claim. It's possible you've never heard of Elisha Gray. With the lawsuit settled and Bell's status as inventor of the telephone established, the popular retelling of the invention moved Gray to a footnote and then, for all intents and purposes, removed him from the story altogether.

We want to believe that seemingly unique inventions and creations are the product of a sole creator. When we have a creative idea, we want the world to recognize us as the genius we are, so we, in turn, recognize others as sole geniuses behind their great ideas. Ideas are kept secret out of fear that they will be stolen. This belief leads to writers mailing themselves copies of their ideas for novels and inventors seeking patents for every small notion they generate. Inside organizations, it leads to departments hiding information or whole projects from the rest of the company. However, it is often the influence of others' ideas that drives our own creative insights. This is as true in technological innovation as it is in fields like literature.

Early in her writing career, Helen Keller stood accused of plagiarism. A story she wrote as an eleven-year-old girl, "The Frost King," had a concept and episodes very similar to those in a story previously published by Margaret Canby. At the center of the controversy was whether or not Keller had read Canby's story before writing her own. Several years later, she received a letter from Mark Twain in which Twain took an aside to explain his perspective on plagiarism accusations, "Oh, dear me, how unspeakably funny and owlishly idiotic and grotesque was that 'plagiarism' farce! As if there was much of anything in any human utterance, oral or written, except plagiarism! . . . For substantially all ideas are second-hand, consciously and unconsciously drawn from a million outside sources, and daily used by the garnerer with a pride and satisfaction born of the superstition that he originated them."[4]

Twain was not a scientist or inventor, but it turns out that his perspective on how innovative ideas develop by building off of one another was quite accurate. There is typically a host of people involved in a new creation, often working independently on what becomes the same discovery. Incidents of nearly simultaneous discovery or invention have a long history. The first comprehensive list of such "multiples" was written in 1922 by William Ogburn and Dorothy Thomas, both sociologists at Columbia University. The list Ogburn and Thomas present contains 148 scientific breakthroughs that could be attributed to multiple people within a similar time frame. Newton and Leibniz both discovered calculus. The telescope was invented by six different people, with Galileo surprisingly the last to figure it out.

Ogburn and Thomas concluded that if so many of the same inventions and discoveries are produced by multiple people, then such multiples must be inevitable. They offered a brief conclusion, arguing that such ideas were the product of the mental ability of inventors and the cultural demand of the time. "If the necessary constituent elements exists," they write, "the invention may occur if there is a cultural need for it."[5] Ogburn and Thomas offered evidence for the old maxim "Necessity is the mother of invention." However, later research implies that creativity and innovation spring from a much more complex set of circumstances than intelligence and need alone.

Economist W. Brian Arthur has been studying the evolution of technology, particularly its influence on building economies, since the 1980s. Arthur builds on the same trend Ogburn and Thomas first wrote about in 1922 to create a full theory of technological development.[6] However, he proposes a more complicated explanation. Arthur notes the apparent similarities between how technology progresses and Darwin's theory of evolution. He also notes a key difference. Whereas Darwin proposed that species evolve through random mutation and natural selection, Arthur asserts that technological developments are not random. Instead of inheriting their genes from biological parents, technologies inherit their parts from the technologies that preceded them. Technologies arise from the combinations of preexisting technologies. These combinations aren't random. Rather, they are the intentional act of the inventor. Arthur calls this "combinatorial evolution." He also observed the exponential effect of combinatorial evolution, that as new technologies are invented, they create more possibilities for combination, and hence the pace of technological innovation quickens.

So how does this explain the phenomenon of multiples? The writer Steven Johnson has been chronicling notable discoveries and famous inventions for years and believes that he has found an explanation. At any given moment, Johnson asserts, there are a finite number of technologies available to be discovered. Although this number may seem incomprehensibly large and growing ever larger in our current age, it is still finite. As each new technology, each novel and useful combination of preexisting ideas, comes into being, it increases the number of possible combinations, but it also increases the number of potential solutions to problems or needs (this is what Ogburn and Thomas theorized was the precursor to invention), creating an opening for a new combination to emerge. To describe that opening, Johnson, in line with Arthur's combinatorial evolution, borrows a concept from biologist Stuart Kauffman regarding evolutionary theory. Kauffman describes how chemical structures sometimes form spontaneously from simpler structures. The structures that form, though, are not totally random. Only those structures that can be made from combining the simpler structures had a likelihood of spontaneous formation. Kauffman called those possible structures the "adjacent possible." Johnson applies this concept to ideas as a whole. He argues that the adjacent possible represents all of the numerous possible combinations and new inventions that could be, but also the finiteness of those combinations at any given time. The adjacent possible dictates the inevitability of certain discoveries.

Johnson's concept of the adjacent possible helps explain the occurrence of multiples. Consider the invention of the telegraph, which sent coded messages as electric pulses through a wire to a receiver who could decode them. Before the telegraph, the idea that human voices and other sounds could be sent through a wire was outside the realm of possibility. The telegraph gave both Bell and Gray a technology to experiment with in solving the problem of sound transmission. It opened up a door to a new possible combination. Bell and Gray were working at the same time with the same materials. That they came across the same successful combination could be said to have been inevitable. Likewise Robert Fulton, the famed innovator of the steam engine, didn't actually invent the device. It had been used in mining for seventy-five years before Fulton figured out how to translate its energy into forward motion and installed it on a ship.[7] When Johannes Gutenberg invented the printing press in 1450, he did so by taking the concept of moveable type and applying it to the already existing technology of the wine press.

Despite the fact that all inventors in a given period of time work with the same materials to achieve sometimes similar results, our tendency is to attribute ownership of an idea to a single person. As we've seen in the history of the telephone, patent law reinforces this tendency by awarding ownership to the person who filed first, even if the time between two similar patents being filed is merely a matter of hours, as in the case of Bell and Gray. Theirs is not the only incident of similar inventions being contested in court, however. Shortly after the invention of the Model T, Henry Ford stood on trial for violating existing patents in his assembly of the automobile. Ford was remarkably blunt when he took the stand and defied the validity of the Originality Myth, his defense an eerie echo of Twain's words to Helen Keller. Ford testified, "I invented nothing new. I simply assembled into a car the discoveries of other men behind whom were centuries of work. . . . Had I worked fifty or ten or even five years before, I would have failed. So it is with every new thing. Progress happens when all the factors that make for it are ready, and then it is inevitable. To teach that a comparatively few men are responsible for the greatest forward steps of mankind is the worst sort of nonsense."[8]

The concept of ideas as combinations of existing materials doesn't apply just to inventions. As we saw with Helen Keller, it can be seen in a variety of creative genres. In literature, Shakespeare's Henry VI plays contain a strong influence from his contemporary Christopher Marlowe's *Tamburlaine the Great*.[9] Marlowe's *Tamburlaine* itself borrows its plot from popular historical books of the time, blended with tales Marlowe had heard from Persia and Turkey. In art, Vincent van Gogh copied the paintings of influential artists of his time, including Emile Bernard, Eugene Delacroix, and Jean-François Millet.[10] All told, more than thirty paintings by van Gogh can be traced back to other original sources. In film, George Lucas's *Star Wars* films are novel combinations of spaghetti westerns, Akira Kurosawa samurai films, and Flash Gordon serials blended together against a borrowed plotline that Joseph Campbell explained in *The Hero with a Thousand Faces*.[11] In advertising, Dan Wieden of Wieden+Kennedy created the infamous Nike slogan "Just Do It" after hearing about the execution of convicted murderer Gary Gilmore.[12] When asked if he had any last words, Gilmore reportedly replied, "Let's do this." Even Walt Disney World, the creative triumph of the legendary animator, can trace its origins to a trip Walt Disney took to Tivoli Gardens in Copenhagen, which featured tamer rides and a family-focused environment.[13]

The theory that new creations are combinations of existing ideas isn't itself a new idea either. Over a hundred years ago, the psychologist Alexander Bain argued that "new combinations grow out of elements already in the possession of the mind."[14] Decades later, another psychologist, Sarnoff Mednick, put forth the similar but further developed idea of "associative thinking." To Mednick, creative thinking was simply "the forming of associative elements into new combinations which either meet specific requirements or are in some way useful."[15] All creative insight was drawn from the ability to connect previous thoughts inside the mind. Therefore, the more connections you could make, the more creative you were. "The greater the number of associations that an individual has to the requisite elements of a problem," Mednick writes, "the greater the probability of his reaching a creative solution."[16] In line with his associationist view, Mednick created the *remote associates test* (RAT) as a measurement of creativity. A RAT works by presenting individuals with a series of seemingly unrelated words and asking them to think of the one word that could be added to each to make a compound word of singular concept. For example, if you were given the three words "arm," "coal," and "peach," the word you'd need to think of would be "pit" (armpit, coal pit, peach pit). The more easily individuals could connect various thoughts in their mind, the more quickly they could solve a RAT question and, Mednick theorized, the more creative they had the potential to be.

Mednick's early theory attempted to describe what was happening inside the mind when creative insights occur, and more recent research is actually looking inside the physical brain. The findings seem to support Mednick's idea. A team of researchers led by Hikaru Takeuchi, a professor of developmental cognitive neuroscience at Tohoku University, have been using sophisticated technology to peek inside the brains of creative people.[17] At the risk of oversimplification, the brain is essentially composed of two types of tissue, commonly called gray matter and white matter. Gray matter is what most people envision when they picture the brain. It's the spongy, wrinkly material that houses all our knowledge, from facts we memorized in grade school to our most prized memories. Gray matter is literally *what* we think about when we think. White matter, in contrast, is the connective tissue that transfers electrical signals across the brain like the wire of a telephone or telegraph. White matter is the wiring that keeps different facts and memories connected. If gray matter is *what* we think, then white matter is *how* we think. When we say that we "forgot" some fact or memory, we still have that memory in our gray matter. It's our white matter that has trouble connecting the thoughts and recalling the information. When we say that we "remembered" something, it generally means that the right connection has been found.

Takeuchi and his colleagues were interested in whether the brains of creative individuals were literally built differently, whether something in their composition of gray and white matter was different than that of less creative individuals. The researchers took a group of participants through a series of exercises designed to measure their divergent thinking ability, a common method for assessing creativity. They then put the participants into an MRI machine and used diffusion tensor imaging to construct a map of their brain, contrasting gray matter and white matter. When the researchers sorted through the brain images and compared those who scored as highly creative to those who scored significantly lower, they found that the physical structures of the brain were in fact different. Creative individuals had significantly more white matter than the less creative comparison group. Literally, their brains were better wired to connect ideas and regions of the brain and potentially produce a creative combination. Takeuchi and his team couldn't say from their research whether these individuals were more creative because of these structures or whether these structures grew as the individuals exercised their creative abilities. A follow-up study led by Takeuchi demonstrated that, with training, it is possible to grow the white matter connections in your brain.[18] The findings hold serious implications for our understanding of creativity. Nearly fifty years after Mednick published his theory that the creative mind works by connecting old ideas in new combinations, brain imaging demonstrated that the brains of those we herald as more creative are in fact better wired to combine ideas. Perhaps more exciting is the suggestion that we can grow the connective tissue in our brains, thus helping enhance our creative ability.

Inventors, marketers, and artists all utilize the raw materials of existing ideas to create new works. The white matter in their brains is constantly connecting and reconnecting ideas, looking for worthwhile combinations. When one or more people create the same combination, we often attribute ownership to the first, or sometimes most famous, person to make the adjacent possible a reality. In doing so, we forget that we are all starting from the same place, with the same available ideas. As Isaac Newton said, "If I have seen further, it is by standing on the shoulders of giants."[19] Indeed, Newton was standing on the shoulders of another giant when he derived that saying from Bernard of Chartres, who originally said, "We are like dwarfs standing on the shoulders of giants, so that we can see more than they."[20]

Newton and Bernard weren't the only ones who stood on the shoulders of giants. One of the most significant innovations of the last hundred years owes its existence to the continued process of older ideas' combining and transforming to create a new and better invention: the personal computer and its easy-to-use operating system. When it was released in 1985, the Windows operating system was a revolutionary innovation. Instead of requiring users to enter scripted commands through a standard keyboard, the Windows system turned a computer screen into a virtual desktop, allowing users to lay out different programs (windows) in order to work on them simultaneously. You could move the windows around and resize them, all by moving a cursor controlled by a "mouse" tethered to the computer. Through its creation, Microsoft has changed the way most humans interact with computers. But that's not the story loyal Apple users will tell you.

Apple loyalists, sometimes called MacHeads, will tell you that Bill Gates and Microsoft copied the most distinctive feature of Windows, known as the graphical user interface (GUI), from the Apple Macintosh.[21] The time lines support their theory. Apple released its Macintosh system in 1984. It featured a mouse and the ability to open programs as different windows, which could be moved around and resized. Although it announced the upcoming release in 1983, Microsoft didn't actually release Windows 1.0 until 1985. While the Macintosh was in development, Apple allowed several people from Microsoft, including Bill Gates, to view the project. Microsoft had contracted to write software for the Macintosh. Steve Jobs, Apple's founder, firmly believed that Windows copied the Mac. Shortly after the introduction of Windows, Jobs confronted Gates about what Jobs thought was a shameless imitation.[22] "You're ripping us off," Jobs reportedly shouted to Gates. "I trusted you and you're stealing from us."

Gates response was much calmer. "Well, Steve," Gates responded. "I think there's more than one way of looking at it. I think it's more like we both had this rich neighbor . . . and I broke into his house to steal the TV set and found out that you had already stolen it." What was Gates referring to? It turns out that a different company had already developed a prototype of the GUI: Xerox.

In 1970, Xerox Corporation launched an ambitious project. It assembled a team of the world's foremost computer engineers and programmers together in a dedicated research facility: the Palo Alto Research Center (PARC). At PARC, the engineers were given an outstanding budget with very little supervision and one goal: to innovate. By 1973, PARC had produced a remarkable machine, the Alto, which was designed to be the world's first personal computer. The Alto featured windows and a mouse-controlled cursor. The device was a huge leap for computing, but it came at a steep cost: $40,000 per computer.

In 1979, Xerox worked out a deal with the up-and-coming Apple and its founder, Steve Jobs. Jobs would let Xerox purchase one hundred thousand shares of Apple stock for only a million dollars (Apple's much-anticipated initial public offering was scheduled for a year later), but only if he were allowed to tour the PARC facility. Jobs was given a few tours, and it was during one of them that he came across the Alto. He was shown how the windows opened and closed and how a mouse could be used to select objects and rearrange them. He was ecstatic. When he returned to Apple, he gathered a team of developers and set them working to create a similar operating system. By 1981, Apple had hired away fifteen developers from Xerox and had them apply their knowledge on two different projects, both of which featured GUIs. In 1984, Apple shipped Jobs's prized Mac. There is still some speculation about what concepts were borrowed and from whom. Apple's Lisa computer, which was under development at the time Jobs toured Xerox, had already planned to incorporate many GUI ideas. Regardless, the Mac operating system looked remarkably like an improved version of the Alto.

So maybe Gates is correct. Maybe Gates and Jobs were both influenced by the Alto. However, the history of the GUI is a bit more complicated than even that. Many of the most creative ideas behind the GUI used by the Alto, the Mac, and Windows were first developed decades beforehand. In 1945, a rudimentary version of the GUI was imagined by Vannevar Bush, an engineer for the U.S. military. In the 1950s, inventor and computer pioneer Douglas Englebart and a team of engineers experimented with Bush's designs at the Department of Defense's Advanced Research Project Agency (ARPA). Before ARPA, Englebart had worked on a project at Stanford developing a mouse.[23] When funding was pulled in the early 1970s, Englebart and his team found a home with Xerox at PARC. The Alto isn't even the first prototype version of an operating system using an interface that could manipulate graphical objects. Credit for that goes to the Sketchpad system, which was the 1963 PhD thesis of Ivan Sutherland at MIT. The Sketchpad had what would later be called icons that could be selected and moved across a screen. The term *icon*, however, comes from the PhD thesis of computer science graduate student David Canfield, who created the on-screen objects for his system, Pygmalion.

It is impossible to trace the GUI found in the Alto, the Macintosh, and Windows back to a single source because there isn't one. Just as Arthur describes, the GUI was designed by combining and modifying preexisting ideas, which themselves were built by combining and modifying even older ideas. Just as with Bell, Gray, and the telephone, the GUI was being worked on by numerous teams of people at numerous different companies at the same time. Parts of the Macintosh operating system were in place before Jobs toured PARC. His visit served to refine some ideas that were already being played with. In addition, in the case of Windows and the Macintosh, both teams made what they felt were improvements on the ideas found in the Alto. The most obvious example: the Alto's mouse had three buttons, Windows' mouse has two buttons, and the Apple mouse has only one.

Jobs even admitted in an interview with *Wired* magazine that his source for innovation was the raw material of old ideas. "Creativity is just connecting things," Jobs said. "When you ask creative people how they did something, they feel a little guilty because they didn't really do it, they just *saw* something. It seemed obvious to them after a while. That's because they were able to connect experiences they've had and synthesize new things. And the reason they were able to do that was that they've had more experiences or they have thought more about their experiences than other people."[24] Ironically, however, even Jobs would invoke the Originality Myth when it suited him. In 2010, in response to the Android mobile phone operating system's similar look and feel to Apple's iOS for iPhone, Jobs threatened, "I am going to destroy Android because it's a stolen product. I'm willing to go thermonuclear war on this."[25] Jobs recognized that great ideas were built from combinations of older ideas, but, paradoxically, he was quick to attack those who built from Apple's ideas.

The story of the GUI perfectly aligns with the truth that innovation comes from combining previously unconnected ideas. It's surprising, then, to see that the current operations and legal structure of so many technology companies are more aligned with the Originality Myth. We know that innovation flourishes when individuals can build from preexisting ideas, but the structures most companies currently employ are designed to build walls, protect secrets, and prevent people outside their circle from using "their" ideas. They do this through a myriad of tactics: patents, trade secrets, digital rights management, and intellectual property laws. All these methods assume that ideas are the property of one person. That assumption carries a large potential cost. If ideas are harder to combine, we will get fewer combinations. If we always demand a single, original creator, we will get less innovation.

It's difficult to trace the origins of almost any innovation or creative work because there are so many different sources. This is the truth behind the Originality Myth. If ideas, creative works, and innovative new technologies are all built from combinations of preexisting material, then we have to admit that it is possible that many people could create the same thing at around the same time. Indeed, this is what happens often. What aids the "original" creators is access to ideas from a variety of sources. As Steve Johnson asserts, every person is also trapped within his or her own adjacent possible. In their creative endeavors, people can only borrow from ideas and materials to which they have been exposed. The more environments and influences they open themselves up to, the wider their adjacent possible is and the more likely they are to stumble across the creative finish line first. The more they can develop their brain's white matter to make connections across gray matter, the greater their potential for a creative insight.

Within organizations, a similar principle applies. The more freedom individuals and teams have to connect and combine ideas, the more likely they are to find an innovative combination, even if those source ideas came from outside their organization. Individuals and organizations thrive when ideas are shared. Not sharing can shrink the adjacent possible of everyone involved. Many people insist on keeping their creative ideas to themselves until they can develop them. They wouldn't want an idea stolen. However, if the idea came from just the right combination among a finite number of possible combinations, then the odds are that someone else will have a similar idea eventually—if he or she hasn't come up with it already. In fact, keeping an idea to yourself may be what keeps it from being developed. Within an organization, clinging to the Originality Myth can lead to individuals and whole departments keeping their insights private. After all, when the project finally launches, we want to make sure our team gets the credit. The truth is that, just like the GUI, when great products and creative works are created, it is often difficult to assign credit to just one person. Sharing insights and combining them in new ways are typically what made them so great in the first place.

The Expert Myth

When facing tough problems that require creative solutions, we often believe that we need to enlist the help of more people with greater expertise. It's why we engage in a rigorous program of study before we set out to make our own mark in the world. It's why the reaction in many organizations to a difficult problem or an inadequate employee is often more training. This is the *Expert Myth*, the belief that a correlation exists between the depth of a person's knowledge and the quality of the work that person can produce. This seems so logical that it's difficult to argue with. In many cases it is even true. Training usually helps, and few would argue that schooling is detrimental. Except that, logical as this seems, the correlation between a person's level of expertise and his or her creative output isn't what one might expect. Research into the lives and careers of creative people shows that, at a certain level, expertise can actually hinder the creative ability of individuals and decrease their creative output. As expertise grows, creativity sometimes diminishes. Sometimes the best insights come from those outside a particular field, and the best inventions develop from teams built from these outsiders.

It was the reliance on a team of those outsiders that helped Jay Martin design and build a revolutionary new prosthetic device. Martin had no experts. As a designer of prosthetic limbs, he received a research grant for $300,000 in 2002 and used it to found his new company, Martin Bionics. The grant was given to help Martin develop a prototype for a new kind of prosthetic ankle. Because our ankles are responsible for so much of the agility required to keep our balance when walking on a changing terrain, prosthetic devices that mimic the ankle can be difficult to develop and fit. Most conventional pros-thetic ankles avoid this problem altogether, focusing solely on what stability can be provided and trusting the user to relearn how to walk accordingly. Martin's idea was to use robotics technology to create a device that would sense the changes in terrain and make adjustments in real time. This hadn't been done before. "Most of the devices that make adjustments are not able to do so in real time," Martin notes. "They can take a reading and make adjustments on the next step, and this is helpful, but it still comes with problems. If you're walking down a ramp that comes to a sudden stop, there are a series of steps that are the same, and those devices work great for that. But when you hit the end of the ramp, you're no longer on an incline. You're on a flat surface, and the device does nothing to help you keep your balance."[1] Martin's proposed ankle would make the real-time adjustments needed in those difficult situations.

Martin's problem wasn't that there were no experts; he had previously employed plenty of them. Upon first receiving the grant, Martin set to work building the best team that could be assembled. He hired a group of PhD-level experts in computer systems and mechanical and electrical engineering. The team began work on the problem but quickly stalled out. Eventually, they concluded that what Martin envisioned could not be done. Every possible solution they thought of had a known barrier they couldn't cross. They argued that the technology wasn't available yet. They argued that the physics didn't work out right. "If it were easily possible," Martin says, "it would have already been done. I knew that going in. I felt it was difficult, but it *was* possible." Martin's team of experts felt otherwise. So he fired them. All of them.

With the slate wiped clean and Martin ready to start again, his new expert problem truly developed: there was money awarded to develop the proposed device and a deadline approaching quickly, but he had no experts who believed that his product could be developed. As part of their basic education, most engineers had learned about the barriers Martin's original team had discovered. "As these engineers and programmers are trained, they run up against all sorts of dilemmas," says Martin. "Some they solve, and others they can't. Especially in prosthetics, the longer you've been working, the more you become certain of what is possible and what isn't." Martin's old team and the existing pool of trained engineers had concluded that what he imagined wasn't possible. So Martin decided to assemble a new team of people who didn't know what wasn't possible.

He addressed the engineering departments of a few local colleges, talking about his life and his current project; at each school, he mentioned that he was looking for interns. Eventually, enough students sought him out, and Martin was able to put together a different kind of team. The eight members of this new team knew the basics of their subject area but had no prior experience in robotics or prosthetics—which meant they had no preconceived notions about the supposed impossibility of their project. They didn't yet know what the barriers to the design were. "They had no conceived notions of what was possible or impossible," Martin recalls. "I told them it was possible, and they believed me. So we got to work."

It took a long time. Martin and his team worked hard through countless cycles of trial and error. It wasn't the most elegant path to success, but eventually they did arrive at a working prototype. The team of layman engineers became the first group ever to develop a real-time control system for a prosthetic ankle of this type. "Had I kept a team of experienced engineers, I might have made progress more steadily, but the product I developed wouldn't have the same quality," Martin argues. "We found a truly creative solution to our development problem, one that a professional-level team might never have discovered."

Martin and his team developed a groundbreaking device. Because of the success of the prosthetic ankle, as well as his other designs for prosthetics, Martin Bionics grew to become one of the largest prosthetics R&D companies in the United States. But Martin never forgot the experience of working with that inexperienced team on that "impossible" project. It led him to realize that his true interest and specialty was in designing new prosthetics, not manufacturing or marketing them. Martin sold his design, and his company, to a prosthetics manufacturer and set his focus entirely on design. "I see inventing like an art form; patents are my canvas," Martin says. His company, now called Martin Bionics Innovations, focuses on designing innovative products in various fields, including prosthetics, using new technologies. And it still hires mostly interns. "Roughly 95 percent of people I hire start as interns. I find I just get a higher level of creativity and drive from them. Their ideas are more innovative, and their solutions more creative."

Martin isn't alone in employing the strategy of using younger interns to generate innovative designs. In an array of fields, younger minds counterintuitively tend to develop the sharpest ideas. In fact, there's a common joke among physics researchers that if you haven't done Noble Prize–winning work by the time you reach the age of thirty, then you should probably move on with your life. To someone outside the discipline, this may seem a little puzzling and quite mean. The longer someone studies a field, we naturally assume, the smarter he or she becomes. Therefore, the older a person gets, the more likely that he or she is to produce breakthrough work. Albert Einstein was awarded the Noble Prize at the age of forty-six, a good number of years past thirty. Examples like his might lead some to believe that the quality of an individual's creative discoveries increases with age. However, Einstein was awarded the prize in 1921 for a body of work that was first published in 1905, his famous *Annus Mirabilis* papers on the photoelectric effect. In addition, his theory of special relativity and discovery of the most famous equation in the world, $E = mc^2$, was also first published in 1905. Einstein was twenty-six when he published his most famous and influential theories. He was well under thirty.

Although it might seem a bit unfair, there's actually some truth to the notion that most physicists hit their peak around thirty years old. And physics isn't the only field with a "young mind" phenomenon. In many domains, creativity and productivity tend to peak fairly early on in a person's career. Yet, with the exception of childhood actors, individuals tend to become much more famous as they age. They earn a larger salary for every year of experience they have. The fame and the larger salary stem from the myth that experience is integral to generating innovative and valuable ideas; however, this conflicts with much of the data on creative careers. For most individuals, the older self is more respected and influential, even if that respect comes from work that the younger self produced. And the older self, while continuing to contribute, is basically accepting a salary that was earned by the younger self's efforts.

The first study of creative output over individual careers was undertaken by the French mathematician Adolphe Quetelet in the early nineteenth century. Quetelet's study was the first to use what is now known as the historiometric method to look at the careers of creative people.[2] The historiometric method attempts to explain human progress or individuals' careers through statistics, such as the amount of work produced in a career and when each work was released. Quetelet studied the careers of English and French playwrights and counted the number of plays each playwright produced year by year over the course of his career. What Quetelet found was that the playwrights' output increased up to a peak age before declining gradually but steadily. If plotted on a graph, their creativity and productivity line would resemble an inverted U. And this was true for the quality of their work as well. As each playwright began his career, he became a factory for scripts, churning out as many as possible with increasing frequency and quality. As the playwrights got older, however, the plays they created didn't get any better. One by one, each playwright in the study wrote fewer plays each year, and, interestingly, the quality of each play also declined. Quetelet found that their best work wasn't done at the end of their career, when presumably they had accumulated the most expertise.

Over the past three decades, the historiometric method has seen a rebirth under Dean Keith Simonton, a professor of psychology at the University of California, Davis. Simonton's work confirms and adds to the original findings of Quetelet. Simonton focused his research on the career age of a variety of creative individuals and found the same inverted-U function. His research shows an increase in productivity up to a certain point, a small plateau during the peak years, and then a gradual decline that continues through the individual's life span, showing that the most productive creatives aren't the seasoned experts with decades of experience. Simonton's research has even confirmed the physicist's warning regarding age. He found that physicists typically make their most influential discoveries before thirty—old enough to understand the basics of the field, but young enough to view those basics with a fresh perspective and to question some of their underlying assumptions. Every domain appears to have its own inverted-U shape, though some are less drastic than others. Social scientists tend to hit their peak productivity in their forties or fifties, humanities scholars in their fifties.

Simonton's thesis is that the level of creative success at a given time in a person's career can be calculated based on that person's ideation rate, the rate at which she generates new configurations of elements and ideas, and her elaboration rate, the rate at which those ideas are experimented on and elaborated into an easier-to-understand form. Both ideation and elaboration rates are important. We need ideation to produce lots of novel ideas, and we need elaboration to find the ones that are also useful. However, it turns out that ideation rate is more important: the higher the quantity of ideas, the higher the likelihood of finding a quality idea. Simonton found that most individuals have a much higher ideation rate earlier in their career, when their thoughts are less organized and their mind makes connections to elements that might at first seem unrelated to their field. As they learn more about their discipline, the ideation rate shrinks. Their expertise might make them better able to judge ideas, but without the large quantity of ideas to draw from, their overall quality and productivity decreases. It could be because they are less willing to embrace and promote ideas that seem more radical. It could also be that they become more constrained by conventional wisdom and the cultural dynamics of their field. So although an expert may have a better or deeper understanding of a body of knowledge, his very depth of knowledge may hinder him from generating more ideas, or it may cause him to dismiss the fringe ideas that could turn out to be the most influential.

Although this peak-age phenomenon is widespread, it is not necessarily inevitable. It is possible to combat a lowering ideation rate and remain productive and influential throughout one's career by adopting the mentality of a young learner, an outsider to the field. This means willingly forcing oneself to entertain nontraditional ideas, setting ideation quotas, and utilizing learned creative thinking skills to generate a greater number of ideas. The easiest possible way to fight the peak-age trend is to become an outsider by entering a brand-new field. Consider the work of Paul Erdos, a mathematician who was known to arrive at the homes of potential collaborators and announce, "My brain is open."[3] He and his collaborators would share knowledge from their respective domains and provide each other with an outsider's perspective. He was frequently moving his own focus from one domain of mathematics to another. As his contribution to one domain was waning, he would set about learning a new domain, benefiting from his outsider's perspective. As a result, Erdos published more mathematical papers than anyone in history, at least 1,525 that we can verify.[4] Erdos's publication record and nomadic reputation even led to what mathematical scholars refer to as the Erdos number, an indication of how far removed one is from Erdos or someone who copublished with him.[5] A mathematician who worked directly with Erdos would have an Erdos number of 1; another who published with someone who had also published with Erdos would have a number of 2; and so on. The Erdos number is a testament to just how productive Erdos's career was and how the source of that productivity was a mind constantly kept fresh with new concepts from new domains.

The evidence suggests that the Expert Myth is riddled with subtle nuances. Sure, most innovations and creative works require a base level of expertise and an ability to work in a specific genre. However, expertise also has the potential to block creative insights. Elite experts, like the ones Jay Martin fired, still produce creative insights, but their expertise can cause them to dismiss those insights in the moment of ideation. In the end, they lack the quantity of new ideas needed to elaborate on so that they can develop the great ones. Paul Erdos, on the contrary, is an example of how keeping one's mind open to new ideas and never too focused on any one area of expertise can fight the peak expertise phenomenon.

Many organizations are following Erdos's strategy on a larger scale, regularly seeking outsiders for new insights without regard to their education or specific expertise. Instead of showing up on the doorstep of one person and announcing that their brains are open, these groups have chosen to open their doors and offer their problems to whoever would like to contribute. The shift these organizations are making toward inviting outside perspectives on difficult problems is producing radical new innovation in everything from what pharmaceuticals are developed to how government operates and even to how we choose what movie to watch next.

In traditional corporations, major technological or product advances typically result from a simple but expensive formula:

firms build massive R&D departments like Bell Labs, Xerox PARC, or the R&D divisions of DuPont or Merck. These firms spend vast sums of money to recruit and retain the top graduates from PhD programs at top universities. Once new recruits sign on, the firms allocate more money for them to spend solving the tough technical problems that accompany groundbreaking developments. Because most organizations seek to grow by deepening the pool of knowledge available inside their own walls, these researchers are paid even more as they gather more experience. It's a system based on the Expert Myth. For much of recent history, this is how innovation happened: inside the well-funded research machines of corporations.

Werner Mueller doesn't work inside any of these organizations. Mueller is a chemist by training who spent much of his working life inside a large multinational chemical company.[6] As he moved through the ranks, however, he found he had to spend more and more time away from the chemistry labs that attracted him to his firm. Finally, when he retired, Mueller built a chemistry lab inside his own home to spend a little time tinkering with his first love.

In late 2001, the research machine of a major pharmaceutical company was beginning to break down, or at least starting to sputter. Despite significant investment in its R&D teams, the company could not find a way around a problem with its potential new product. The company had found a relatively inexpensive but powerful compound, but the process involved in making that compound into a marketable drug was enormously inefficient, which kept adding to the final cost of the drug. Over budget and out of ideas, the research team posted their problem anonymously online, which is how the problem got moved from the rich research labs of the company to the home chemistry set of Werner Mueller. Although Mueller hadn't worked in the pharmaceutical industry, he recognized the problem as something similar to one he experienced in his career as an industrial chemist. So he went to work trying to discover a solution. Eventually, Mueller felt that he'd found a method that he thought could be useful, and submitted the potential solution to the company. The research team hadn't considered his solution before, and when it was tested, it worked brilliantly. The pharmaceutical company had its drug, and Mueller had a $25,000 prize to reinvest in his home-based chemistry lab. Mueller now spends his retirement inside his prized lab, working on solutions to various problems posted on a website called InnoCentive.

InnoCentive is a nontraditional approach to innovation that was truly born out of necessity. It works a bit like an eBay for problem solving. The website was launched in 2001 by Alpheus Bingham, then a vice president at pharmaceutical giant Eli Lilly, the very company whose problem Mueller had solved. Bingham was frustrated with the traditional R&D model: finding the smartest people available and giving hard problems to them. The issue wasn't the people or the problems; it was the combination of the two. Bingham had no way of knowing whether the right people were being assigned to the right problems. The traditional assumption was to try to match the brightest person to the hardest problem, but as we've seen, sometimes being the expert can put one at a disadvantage.

Bingham launched the InnoCentive project as a last resort. He couldn't spend more money on the same failed solutions, and he didn't know where to allocate resources. He didn't know how solvable certain problems were or how long they would require to solve, which made internal planning nearly impossible. But if the problem was being worked on externally, with a fixed prize for finding a working solution, then the budget and resource planning came much more easily. At first the response was slow, and Bingham began to wonder if his project was worth the money spent on developing the site. But eventually solutions started coming in. Mueller's solution was among those submitted. It solved not just the research team's problem of developing the compound but also Bingham's problem of managing an expensive R&D dilemma.

In 2003, the InnoCentive project was spun off from Lilly as an independent company, with Bingham still at the helm as its CEO. The website posts problems from hundreds of corporations (called "seekers") like DuPont, Boeing, Novartis, and Procter & Gamble. The range of problems is diverse, from designing lithium-ion batteries to developing reduced-fat chocolate alternatives. The range of individuals working on these problems (called "solvers"), however, is even more diverse. Over two hundred thousand people have registered with InnoCentive as potential problem solvers. This, Bingham believes, is the real reason the site works. "It produces a diversity of thought about the problem that can often make the solution rather unique."[7] This diversity of thought is precisely where the solutions come from. Most problem solvers on InnoCentive solve problems that aren't related to their traditional domain. Instead, the problems solved are often at the fringes of a solver's expertise. Just as Werner Mueller was trained as an industrial chemist and solved a pharmaceutical problem, the majority of solutions come from individuals whose training brings them close enough to understand a problem's complexity, but not too close to limit their range of thinking when it comes to possible solutions.

InnoCentive isn't the only route companies are using to open themselves up to the creativity of nonexperts. In 2006, Netflix began a widely publicized competition for its Netflix Prize.[8] The DVD and streaming movie company was looking to improve the quality of its recommendation algorithm, which offers users suggestions for movies to watch in the future based on movies they've watched and rated in the past. Instead of spending time and resources in-house, the company decided it would be more efficient to tap into the potential of everyone willing, regardless of his or her background or employer. For the competition, the company asked contestants to design a new algorithm that would improve the quality of recommendations by at least 10 percent. Netflix would test that algorithm by asking it to make predictions from a sample of its actual customers. Netflix offered $1 million to the team that could reach the 10 percent improvement threshold first. In addition to the grand prize, the company also offered "progress prizes" of $50,000 each year to the team that had the best results to date, in order to encourage ongoing commitment and even collaboration among the teams.

After three years and submissions from forty thousand teams in 186 countries, Netflix awarded its grand prize to an unlikely assortment of contestants in 2009. The team, creatively named BellKor's Pragmatic Chaos, was a cadre of statisticians, artificial intelligence experts, and computer engineers from the United States, Canada, Austria, and Israel. Their algorithm improved on the method Netflix was using at the time by 10.06 percent, the first submission to cross that finish line. Interestingly, the seven-member team actually began the competition as three separate teams. Over the course of three years, as each team saw the others' progress and insights, they decided to merge in order to collectively benefit from everyone's unique perspectives. The first time the team members met in person was when they arrived at Netflix to claim their prize.

In a surprising twist, Netflix never actually implemented the team's algorithm in its business. Over the duration of the contest, the focus of the company's business model had moved from DVDs by mail to Internet movie streaming, a shift that required a different algorithm. Although over $1 million might seem like an extraordinary price to pay for an unused improvement, Netflix did directly implement some improvements inspired by an earlier submission for a progress prize. In addition, watching the teams compete and make progress provided some important lessons for the company on the best process to improve its algorithms in the future.

InnoCentive and the Netflix Prize demonstrate the power of what is commonly called crowdsourcing, seeking out a large crowd of outsiders to help solve complex problems. But similar innovative power can be seen with a much smaller number of outsiders, sometimes just one, and even on much more complex problems, like the ones faced in government. One nonprofit,

Fuse Corps, is working to recruit and train entrepreneurial professionals and pair their outsider perspectives with civic leaders in need of innovative ideas.

The Fuse Corps program identifies projects in communities throughout the United States that address a national priority, such as education, health care, or economic development. "It started as a random idea," explains Fuse Corps cofounder Lenny Mendonca.[9] "I spent a lot of time on the board at the Stanford business school, and I saw an enormous thirst in the students for doing something of value, but a disconnect in how they could do that." The traditional path of a business school student is to take on loads of debt during school and then compete for the highest-paying job in industries like consulting or finance to pay off those debts. Even if the students wanted to make an impact, the system was set up to focus and train them to make a profit. "At the same time, I kept having conversations with leaders in the public sector," Mendonca says. "Mayors and governors have really interesting problems, but they can't find the right people to help solve those problems. If we can take the creativity that is fueling innovation in the private sector and apply it to social capital, we'd see drastic gains in social progress."

Fuse Corps took on the challenge of pairing these leaders with a selected entrepreneur or midcareer professional to collaborate on the project. "What's your transformational goal? We'll get you the right person," Fuse Corps cofounder and CEO Jennifer Anastasoff says to potential civic leaders looking for Fuse Corps fellows.[10] The goal has to be specific and measurable, with a definite impact on the community and a direct influence on civic leaders. Fuse Corps then identifies a match from its pool of applicants. Every potential applicant must have at least eight years of professional, private sector experience, and experienced entrepreneurs are preferred. The right candidate will have a demonstrated commitment to service but does not need any prior expertise in the particular area of his or her fellowship. "Fellows don't start by presuming that they have all the answers by looking at problems from a bird's eye view," says another of the program's cofounders, Peter Sims.[11] "Rather, they begin from the worm's eye view by developing greater empathy for citizens, their problems and needs, then build up to new solutions."

In 2012, Noelle Galperin spent the majority of her time working to raise awareness and support for the Oakland, California–based child advocacy group Children Now and its efforts to build the Children's Movement of California, a coalition of organizations focused on helping give children an opportunity to reach their full potential. Although Galperin is no stranger to hard work or service, working with the Children's Movement was a change from her typical working day. "No two days have been the same for me since I started," she notes.[12] "But as an entrepreneur, that's the kind of environment I thrive in." Galperin holds an MBA from Harvard and has twenty years of experience in operational marketing and strategic management. She took a sabbatical from her established consulting practice to work with the Children's Movement, and spent her yearlong tenure forging alliances with various groups that support children's issues and developing an overall government strategy to ensure the advancement of a long-term agenda for children. Her work put her elite business education and entrepreneurial thinking at the crossroads between non-profit institutions and elected officials, and brought some much-needed innovation to both camps.

"The fellows are all working on mission-critical initiatives at our organizations that have not been adequately resourced," Galperin explains.[13] "Thus one of our tasks is to find creative ways to access appropriate resources to build those initiatives to a point where they're receiving the investment necessary to continue developing and creating impact for the organization and beyond." The combination of entrepreneurial thinking and civic engagement to drive innovation in the host communities has already shown dramatic results for each of the Fuse Corps fellows.

Laurel Lichty put her international energy law practice on hold to work with the Delaware secretary of education to promote and measure the state's progress toward federal Race to the Top educational development goals and to ensure continuous improvement. Erika Dimmler, an experienced television producer, took a yearlong leave of absence from CNN to work with Mayor Kevin Johnson and the City of Sacramento to bring Alice Waters's Edible Schoolyard project to the Sacramento Unified School District and enhance the quality of its students' education, and their lunches. Lisa Gans joined the executive leadership team of nonprofit start-up DC Promise Neighborhood Initiative and helped create a five-year strategic plan for the group and even helped it receive a $25 million grant to fund its efforts to improve the health, safety, and quality of life for children in poor neighborhoods of Washington, DC. Before joining Fuse Corps, Gans was a corporate and human rights attorney who helped write new constitutions in Iraq and Swaziland. Former strategy consultant and nonprofit executive Jeremy Goldberg spend 2012 working in San Jose's Silicon Valley Talent Partnership, an initiative that pairs top-level private sector individuals with government agencies who need assistance from the rich talent pool of Silicon Valley. "A lot of problems that need to be solved involve the intersection of the private, public, and nonprofit sectors," says Lenny Mendonca, who is also a senior partner and director at McKinsey & Company.[14] "Fuse Corps deliberately selects host organizations and fellows that will let those domains intersect." So far, bringing together the fresh perspectives of private sector executives and the experts inside the public and social sectors is having a drastically positive effect on social innovation.

Efforts like InnoCentive, the Netflix Prize, and Fuse Corps have been so successful because they tap into the evidence that dispels the Expert Myth. Where creativity is concerned, it's possible to become too engrained in a single domain and be too much of an expert. The Expert Myth argues that the hardest problems are solved by the brightest minds in the field, but the evidence counters with a different argument. The people who solve tough problems often come from the edge of a domain. They have enough knowledge to understand the problem but don't have a fixed method of thinking. Because of this, they possess the creative ability to find the right solution. Their unique perspective allows them to generate a diverse set of ideas and still have enough domain knowledge to evaluate which ideas have merit.

Not every organization can hand over every problem to the masses of potential online solvers or offer a one-year fellowship to bring help from an outsider, but they can still leverage the hidden talent of outsider perspectives. Building teams of people from diverse backgrounds, or at least encouraging the sharing of problems across functional teams, should allow for more perspectives on the problem and more potential solutions. In addition, moving people around to various divisions, which is similar to the method Paul Erdos employed to stay productive and keep his brain open, brings the benefit of their old perspective to their new division. Regardless of the method chosen, the key to combating the Expert Myth is to avoid functional fixedness and force ourselves to understand old problems in new ways.

The Incentive Myth

Traditionally, if you want something done by another person, you can simply commission it. In business, the most obvious example of this is the hiring of people who are paid to work on specific tasks. For particularly important tasks, incentives are built in to increase employees' motivation. There's even an old saying spoken in countless Principles of Management classrooms: "If you want something done in business, measure it. If you want something done well, monetize it." This method has its roots in the early management practices of the industrial era; individuals were hired to complete specific tasks inside a highly structured factory. As the economy grew, despite its shift from industry to information, the old methods clung on, even in regard to managing creative work. That we commission and reward creative work the same way we do industrial work is part of the *Incentive Myth*, which is the larger notion that the output and quality of creativity can be increased with incentives. This is how the majority of for-profit businesses and even many nonprofit organizations work. But many organizations are departing from the Incentive Myth. These organizations have found little correlation between creative work and the size of an incentive. Instead, these companies and nonprofit groups alike are seeking out talented individuals and finding ways to encourage their creative genius without traditional incentives.

Jad Abumrad is one such creative genius. At least, that's what most people label him ever since he was awarded a MacArthur Fellowship in 2011. Abumrad is the creator of *Radiolab*—a radio program syndicated through National Public Radio—which he hosts with cocreator Robert Krulwich. *Radiolab* does not feel like a typical radio show. Each episode focuses around a concept, typically scientific or philosophical in nature. Each episode is elaborately stylized, blending together expert interviews and host dialogue with music and sound effects to create a unique listening experience. Abumrad, who majored in music composition at Oberlin College, started the show as a collaboration between himself and Krulwich. Their first major project was an audio experiment for *This American Life* that they created in 2003, but that never made it to air. The two refined their collaboration, and *Radiolab* launched its first official season on New York Public Radio in 2005. Six years later, Abumrad's first hint that he might win the MacArthur award came in the form of a vague email sent by the MacArthur Fellows Program director at the time, Daniel J. Socolow. Abumrad says that his first reaction was that he'd received a scam email, but in later conversations with Socolow, the reality of the award set in.

The MacArthur Fellowship is a grant given to individuals who are believed to have exceptional creative potential. Currently, the award is a five-year stipend of $100,000 per year. The recipients are chosen based not just on the creativity of their past work but on how that work demonstrates potential for future advances. The fellowship focuses on labeling its recipients as exceptionally creative, but most people in the media refer to the award as the "genius grant." The MacArthur Foundation disagrees with this label, finding the concept of "genius" too limiting. Genius is a measurement of intelligence alone; what MacArthur seeks is creativity. Just as *Radiolab* episodes differ from traditional radio programs, the MacArthur Fellows Program is not run like your average grant program. In a traditional grant program, individuals or teams apply for a grant by completing a lengthy proposal outlining what funding they need, what they plan to do with the funding, and the results they expect to achieve. When a project is funded, there is an expectation that it will yield these results with very few surprises. The MacArthur Fellowship is different in two key ways.

The first is that MacArthur Fellows do not apply for a fellowship or grant. There is no specific proposal. Instead, they are nominated anonymously by a pool of people that the MacArthur Foundation keeps even more confidential than its list of nominees. The secret pool of nominators is ever changing. Nominators are chosen based on their expertise and familiarity with exceptionally creative people in their respective fields. Winners do not even know they were being considered until they are selected. Abumrad says that he was totally unaware of his nomination or selection when Socolow called him to verify the news. According to Abumrad's account, Socolow almost teased him, asking if he'd known anyone who had won the award.[1] "I'll give you a hint," Socolow reportedly told Abumrad, "Their name starts with an A. The next letter is B. And the next letter is a U," at which point Abumrad caught on.

The MacArthur Fellowship differs from traditional grants in another, more significant way. The $500,000 stipend is awarded with no strings attached and no obligation to spend the money in a certain manner. According to its website, "The MacArthur Fellowship is designed to provide seed money for intellectual, social, and artistic endeavors. We believe that highly motivated, self-directed, and talented people are in the best position to decide how to allocate their time and resources."[2] The fellowship is designed to provide maximum freedom for recipients to follow their creative impulses. "It totally reverses the normal funder-recipient relationship," Socolow told the *Harvard Business Review* in 2007.[3] Instead of committing its grant recipients to specific projects that had to be approved ahead of time, MacArthur trusts that the award will be best used if the foundation steps back from the process entirely and gives its fellows maximum freedom to create.

The inspiration for this unique program has its roots in the very founding of the MacArthur Foundation. The foundation was started in 1978 upon the death and endowment of John D. MacArthur, a wealthy Chicago businessman. MacArthur chose the original board but provided no guidelines for it to follow. In one of its first meetings, the board began discussing an article by Dr. George Burch titled "Of Venture Research." Burch's argument was that money should be awarded to researchers differently than was being done at the time. Burch believed that creative individuals should be given the freedom to think and act without having to convince an organization to fund them.[4] In 1981, the board awarded its first set of stipends, and the tradition of the no-strings-attached MacArthur Fellowship was born. Since its inception, MacArthur has awarded stipends to an increasingly diverse set of fellows, including scientists, poets, historians, physicians, novelists, nonprofit leaders, musicians, anthropologists, and the aforementioned radio show host. Although the foundation does not require specific products or even reports from its fellows on what they've done since being awarded the stipend, the fellows have put their grants to good use writing new literary works, expanding their own research projects, funding programs that provide modular housing to the urban poor, and even remodeling an ancient monastery to serve as an international artists' residence.

The MacArthur Fellowship stands in opposition to the traditional process of nonprofit funding, but it also finds itself outside our commonly held beliefs about creativity, incentives, and productivity. Fortunately, many organizations appear to be taking cues from the MacArthur Fellows Program and have begun experimenting with a different model. In line with the research on creativity in the workplace, these organizations are experimenting with different methods for enhancing creative productivity. They're moving away from the industrial era thinking that inspired the Incentive Myth and moving toward new practices that stimulate employees to think more creatively. These new practices are having a dramatic effect on innovation.

During the height of the industrial era, the captains of industry were beginning to have problems with their crews. Factory work is often repetitive; the same series of tasks is repeated every few minutes, every hour, day after day. It was hard to keep individuals motivated to perform those tasks quickly and efficiently. At least until Frederick Taylor, the father of management science, did something about it. A factory manager and mechanical engineer by training, Taylor developed a system that he believed would better manage industrial labor. He argued that if people found work dull and unmotivating, the best way to improve performance was to attach a monetary incentive to it. Workers would become motivated by the prospect of earning more money. In the early 1900s, when Taylor was experimenting, much of the work he studied was industrial work, which lent itself to this incentive scheme. As society developed, however, the tools Taylor proposed did not. For a long time this wasn't an issue. Throughout the twentieth century, as more Americans traded in their factory overalls for button-down shirts, much of the work they were doing was still repetitive and routine. Especially in the lower levels of an organization, most white-collar work was still something that involved a little training and a lot of repetition. Taylor's methods of using monetary incentives to inject motivation into these roles still seemed effective.

But creative work is different. In the work Taylor wrote about, there were usually clearly spelled-out instructions, and the task was to follow those to the letter. In creative work there are no spelled-out instructions, and the tasks to follow have to be discovered first. This type of work is becoming more prevalent. According to a recent study by the consulting firm McKinsey & Company, close to 70 percent of job growth in the United States comes in the form of jobs for which instructions aren't known and problems still need solutions.[5] These jobs call for creativity instead of repetitiveness. There is no routine, and there is often plenty of motivation inherent in the work itself. The presence of this inherent motivation makes Taylor's ideas ineffective.

Research on the role of incentives in creative work has been undertaken for almost as long as research on creativity itself. Some of the finer points are still being worked out, but the field is moving toward consensus on a few important issues. Motivation is one of the biggest influencers of creative expression; recall that it is one of Teresa Amabile's four components of individual creativity. As individuals become more motivated to solve problems or engage in creative work, the likelihood of an innovative solution increases. However, the type of motivation present seems to matter almost as much as whether or not it is present at all. Motivation comes in two forms, intrinsic and extrinsic. Intrinsic motivation comes from inside ourselves; it is the desire to complete a task for the simple enjoyment of the task. When we are naturally interested in our work, engrossed in it while we do it and thinking about it even when we're not, we are intrinsically motivated. Extrinsic motivation is the opposite. It is motivation that comes from outside ourselves—like an incentive. When we complete a task for some reason other than the task itself—say, a bonus check or a good grade—we are extrinsically motivated. As the research on motivation and creativity piles up, it appears to be leaning toward a conclusion: intrinsic motivation results in far more creative work than extrinsic motivation.

In one of the more popular studies that demonstrate this conclusion, a team of researchers led by Amabile examined the creativity of artists when working on pieces they chose to create as opposed to their creativity when working on commissioned pieces.[6] Amabile and her team assembled a group of twenty-three painters and sculptors and asked them to choose twenty pieces of art they had created, ten of which they had been commissioned to create and ten of which they had created for the simple joy of practicing their art. The researchers took the 460 total works and displayed them to a panel of art experts, from museum curators to gallery owners to other artists. The panel was asked to rate the quality of each piece. They were not told who created the pieces or which pieces were created for money and which were not. They were just told to assess each piece individually. When the researchers calculated the rating results, they found that those pieces that artists had been commissioned to create were rated as significantly lower in quality than those pieces the artists created for the love of working on them. Although it's certainly possible that the artists working on commissioned pieces had some level of intrinsic motivation while at work, it's also possible that the presence of a payment for the work could have negated some of their intrinsic motivation, which in turn had a negative effect on the overall quality of the piece. This study demonstrates what Amabile calls the intrinsic motivation principle of creativity: "Intrinsic motivation is conducive to creativity; controlling extrinsic motivation is detrimental to creativity."[7] Amabile's explanation is that when extrinsic motivators like incentives are present, they divert the attention of the individual away from the work itself—there is too much focus on thinking of the money and not enough focus on creating. Think of how the artists in the study could focus entirely on their work when creating for themselves but also had to consider the demands and desires of clients for the pieces that were commissioned. Amabile's thesis is supported by forty years of research from another psychologist, Edward Deci, who found that the presence of certain extrinsic rewards could actually remove the intrinsic motivation that was already present in an individual.[8] In certain conditions, incentives can actually block the motivation we need to do creative work.

This doesn't mean that people should never be compensated for their creative work. We all need a level of compensation substantial enough to avoid being distracted by our financial situation and to allow us instead to focus on being creative. Structuring that compensation for creative work is just more difficult than Frederick Taylor could have predicted. However, incentive and reward systems can be designed to avoid dampening intrinsic motivation. Amabile has even suggested that extrinsic motivators are not always detrimental; they just need to be in line with the intrinsic reasons for completing a task.[9] Incentives that aren't perceived as a direct controlling mechanism—a carrot or a stick—can actually enhance intrinsic motivation. Incentives or rewards that are used as a form of recognition for quality performance seem to increase intrinsic interest in creative work. Moreover, rewards that enable people to work on something they are naturally interested in have an even greater effect.

Think about the MacArthur Fellows Program, which offers a monetary prize based on past creative work. The fellowship itself is a form of recognition, and the stipend allows the recipient to choose what to work on in the future. The MacArthur Foundation is adamant in emphasizing that the money is not a reward for past work, however. Instead, it views the fellowship as an incentive, as a means of encouraging even more creative work from its fellows. The award is an extrinsic motivator that is aligned with the fellows' intrinsic motivation. Obviously, it's difficult for an organization to copy the MacArthur Fellowship model. Few consultants would advise their clients to hand out sums of cash and trust that their employees will return the favor by pursuing creative work that will help the company turn a profit. However, some organizations have begun experimenting with something like the MacArthur model on a much smaller scale. These companies are giving "genius grants" to their people in the form of time off to tinker with intrinsically motivating projects and rewarding them when that work helps the company.[10]

The most famous of these "tinker time" programs can trace its history all the way back to 1925 and a man named Dick Drew. At the time, Drew was selling sandpaper.[11] He worked for a fairly large industrial products company, and his main job was traveling around demonstrating the effectiveness of his company's sandpaper products. Drew's work took him to a lot of auto body shops, where he noticed that most of these shops shared a common problem. When they were done making their repairs, shop workers would have to repaint the body of a car. If the car they were painting was two-tone, it was particularly difficult to repaint perfectly. Usually the shop team would paint the car entirely one color and then apply sheets of butcher paper to the places that they wanted to protect so that they could paint the rest of the car a second color and create a two-toned paint job. It was a smart process, but it had a flaw. When they removed the tape, it would remove some of the first coat of paint with it. The adhesive they were using was just too strong. They then had to repaint the damaged sections by hand, adding several man-hours to the job.

Drew's mind made a connection between the taped butcher paper on these cars and the sandpaper samples in his briefcase. Sandpaper is basically a combination of two elements, sticky paper and an abrasive. Glue is applied to one side of the paper and then dipped in crushed minerals. If the abrasive was never applied, however, the product was simply paper with a moderate adhesive on one side—which was similar to what these shop workers needed. When Drew returned to his office, he began to experiment with his sandpaper. It turned out that the glue used to make sandpaper, though weaker than what the body shops were using, was still too strong to help them. So he began to tinker with the glue's formula, trying to weaken the adhesive. Once he found the right adhesive formula, he still had another problem to solve: how to apply it to the paper properly. Without the addition of the abrasive, the paper had one sticky side exposed, which made it hard to package and sell, as the sheets would just end up sticking to each other.

It was around this time that Drew's manager intervened. Drew's boss, William McKnight, saw that Drew had spent a significant amount of company time over several months and had only produced a sticky paper that clumped to itself. McKnight ordered Drew to stop working on the project. McKnight saw the company as a sandpaper company, and told Drew that he needed to sell sandpaper or find another company to work for. Drew didn't listen. He stopped working on the project during company time but would often stay at work to continue his experiments long after everyone else left. Eventually, he found the solution to his packaging problem. Because the paper was only slightly sticky, it could be rolled up on itself like ribbon, and pieces separated from the roll when they were needed. Within less than a year of his initial idea, Drew had invented masking tape. Drew's product didn't just appeal to auto body shop workers looking for a better way to paint cars. It turned out that nearly everyone had a use for removable tape. Within three years of Drew's initial idea, his company, 3M, was selling more of Drew's tape than its sandpaper products.

McKnight never forgot how Drew had ignored his order to stop working on the project. He didn't punish Drew. Instead, he eventually reorganized the entire company around Drew's creative deviance. Shortly after he became president of the company in 1929, McKnight created a new policy: 3M's technical staff could spend up to 15 percent of their time working on projects of their own choosing without needing approval from their supervisors.[12] The rule became known as 3M's "bootlegging policy" and is still in place today. According to the former head of R&D for 3M, most of the company's core products emerged from time spent by bootlegging engineers.[13] Spencer Silver and Art Fry's aforementioned invention of the Post-it Note in Chapter Two, for example, was made possible through the time allotted to them to bootleg. Although McKnight's policy predates the MacArthur Fellowship, it bears a striking resemblance to the philosophy behind the program.

Following in the footsteps of 3M, an increasing number of companies are experimenting with giving their employees "genius grants" of free time to work on intrinsically motivating projects instead of incentivizing them to do the work assigned to them. Australian software company Atlassian began to give its people twenty-four hours every quarter for such activity.[14] Employees could work on whatever project they desired as long as it was outside the realm of normal work and as long as they committed to sharing their results the next day. Their experiments with free time generated numerous software bug fixes and product ideas. In fact, the program was so successful that Atlassian adopted a formal policy of giving employees 20 percent of the workweek for bootlegging time.[15]

Innovation powerhouse W. L. Gore uses a method similar to 3M but gives people slightly less bootlegging time. At Gore, associates reserve 10 percent of their time to pursue new, speculative projects. In fact, the Elixir guitar string project mentioned in Chapter Three actually began as a 10 percent time project for Dave Myers and two other Gore colleagues.[16] They eventually convinced six other associates to join them, and after three years of working on the guitar strings as a side project, the team finally proposed the idea to the rest of the organization and transformed it into an official project. The same 10 percent of company time is allotted to scientists at Corning, a glassware company. At Corning's Sullivan Park R&D lab, scientists reserve 10 percent of their workweek for "Friday afternoon experiments" to pursue ideas that might seem slightly crazy.[17] Scientists use the time to pursue offbeat ideas under the radar of their managers and also to resurrect projects their bosses might have killed.

The social media company Twitter holds regular "hack weeks": employees are given an entire week to pursue an interesting project that is outside the regular domain of their job. Many work on new software fixes, but any project is fair game. For example, a few folks banded together and created a low-fi but hilarious recruiting video that quickly went viral. The hack week concept was so successful at Twitter that founder Jack Dorsey took it with him when he founded the payment processing company Square. At Square, hack week has birthed a wealth of great projects. The extension application Square Wallet, which makes it possible to pay vendors using only a smartphone, began as a hack week project, as did a wireless receipt printing method. But whimsical projects aren't off-limits either. One hack week, a team developed an application that allows Square employees to monitor the company pool table to see if it's taken or available for play. Another engineer figured out how to install a prepaid cellular phone inside a hollowed-out banana. Although it's easier to calculate the return on investment from a project like Square Wallet, the pool table app or banana phone project is just as important for inspiring and developing employees' creativity. Often during hack week, employees with great ideas but no experience in programming learn the coding skills they need to turn those ideas into valuable product fixes or extensions. So what if that learning happened while rigging up a video camera to monitor the pool table?

At Facebook, employees gather once a month for twelve-hour "hack-a-thons."[18] Everyone in the company is invited to pull a collective all-nighter from 8 PM to 8 AM, during which he or she experiments with new projects. There are only two rules for participating in a hack-a-thon. The first is that the projects cannot be part of the person's regular work. The second is that the next morning, individuals or teams have to deliver a brief presentation about what they worked on and what they accomplished during their hack. Hundreds of people participate every month, and the morning is filled with presentations. Some people spend the night coding new applications. Facebook Chat began its life as a hack-a-thon project and eventually became a full-time job for its hacker. Others spend their time on experiments that seem less than useful at first. One team decided to hack an identification card reader and attach it to a keg of beer. When someone swiped her Facebook credentials, the card reader took a picture and posted it as a status update on the user's Facebook profile before allowing her to pour a beverage. Even though the idea seemed pointless to the hackers at first, those who saw their presentation the next morning found the technology useful for places other than bars. A similar technology is now being utilized at conferences and trade shows, where attendees swipe their name badges at vendor booths or other stations and the reader updates their status on Facebook.

Perhaps no company has taken the idea of autonomous work time further than 37signals, a software company that makes Web-based applications for businesses. In June 2012, 37signals announced that it would be giving all of its employees an extended stretch of time—an entire month—to experiment on whatever they wanted.[19] Employees set aside everything in their normal work schedule except customer service and server maintenance. Although it took a few days for employees to adjust to their newfound autonomy, eventually they started tinkering with new ideas. Some worked solo for the entire month; others formed teams immediately or as the need for extra help arose. On July 11, the company reunited for "Pitch Day," during which everyone shared the results of the monthlong experiment. One team presented a set of new customer service tools that was quickly appreciated and accepted. Another team developed a data visualization technique for better analyzing the way customers interact with the company's products. They solved the challenging problem of how to make their wealth of user data a source of insight. Not all pitches were accepted, but all of them were a source for new, innovative ideas. Jason Fried, cofounder of the company, has already resolved to make these experiments a regular part of how 37signals works. "How can we afford to put our business on hold for a month to 'mess around' with new ideas?" Fried writes, anticipating the most common question. "How can we afford not to? We would never have had such a burst of creative energy had we stuck to business as usual."[20] Fried continues, "If you can't spare some time to give your employees the chance to wow you, you'll never get the best from them."

In the traditional approach to managing employees, your people are paid to complete specific tasks, not to tinker with new ideas. Even when individuals in artistic industries are "commissioned," there is usually a specific product the commissioner is expecting. These traditions are rationalized through the assumption that the higher the incentive, the better the work. They rely on the Incentive Myth. But programs like the MacArthur Fellowship are unique in that they don't ask for a specific project before awarding someone funding. The monetary stipend is beneficial, but the biggest benefit comes from the autonomy awarded by the foundation to its fellows. What many for-profit companies, from 3M to Twitter, share with the MacArthur Fellows Program is a belief that if they can identify talented, creative people with a track record of quality work, then they're better off allowing those people to work autonomously on projects that are intrinsically motivating. There is risk to this process, just as there is risk that giving $500,000 to a lone "genius" won't yield a single quality work. However, the research supports that the risk is well worth it. These organizations believe that the opposite approach, wasting money on incentive programs to produce artificial motivation and poorer-quality work, is even riskier.

The Lone Creator Myth

We have a tendency to favor stories of one person against the entire world. We likewise tend to attribute creative works or innovative ideas to one lone creator, even when that person isn't solely responsible. We love to imagine the starving poet slaving away in his sparse apartment, the genius painter who keeps her artwork so closely guarded that it rarely makes it into shows before her death, or the heroic inventor working with nothing but his intelligence and a pile of junk. We might accept that outside influences helped inspire creators, but we tend to view the act of creation as a lonely endeavor. This is the *Lone Creator Myth*. It's the belief that creativity is a solo performance and that the story of innovations can be told as the story of a single person working fervently on the new idea. In the popular media, this myth sells. Magazines, newspapers, and books are filled with stories of lone creative geniuses. These stories tend to ignore a truth behind all great innovations and creative works: those geniuses typically had teams. But only rarely is consideration given to the larger team or network those individuals were connected to, and often even then it is a footnote in the "soloist's" story.

Once we realize that creativity is a team effort and understand how to develop the most creative teams, we can generate even more great ideas. Too often, however, we prefer to recognize only one person for an outstanding creative work. This isn't just a selective revision; it's a fabrication. The story of one of the most famous inventions, the invention we use as a symbol of innovation, involves just such a fabrication.

Thomas Edison didn't try ten thousand times before inventing the lightbulb.

That notion is false on three different fronts. Edison didn't invent the lightbulb so much as he refined it. There weren't ten thousand attempts to find the right filament to use in the lightbulb, and, perhaps most important, it really wasn't Edison doing all that trying. The story of Edison alone in a workshop experimenting with ten thousand different materials isn't true even though it was most likely first told by Edison himself. Edison may have spread this story to help sell his invention, but the story's popularity has caused it to become a potentially dangerous myth.

In tracing the origin of the lightbulb, historians Robert Friedel and Paul Israel compiled a list of twenty-two people who invented incandescent lamps before Edison even filed his first patent for a lightbulb.[1] John W. Starr, who filed a caveat for a U.S. patent in 1845 but died shortly afterward, was among those who preceded Edison.[2] When Edison filed his first patent related to electric lamps, it was rejected because the patent office felt that it infringed on Starr's preexisting patent. After making a few adjustments to his design, Edison filed a patent titled "Improvement in Electric Lights" in 1878. At the time, however, the right filament was still an unsettled issue.

Depending on the source, Edison tested seven hundred, one thousand, six thousand, ten thousand, or some other number of filaments before finding the perfect materials. According to the Smithsonian, Edison tested sixteen hundred different filaments—everything from coconut fiber to human hair—before settling on carbonized bamboo fiber.[3] It's difficult to know the exact number of attempts, however, as much of the exaggeration was circulated by Edison himself when speaking to the press. Edison told of a worldwide search for the perfect fiber in order to advertise the rigor of his invention process and the superiority of his new lightbulb.[4] Moreover, whatever materials were actually tried, it's highly likely that Edison wasn't the one experimenting with them. The bulk of Edison's work on electric lightbulbs came as a result of his greatest invention: Menlo Park.

Edison got his start in the telegraph industry, where he created numerous improvements to the telegraph and generated some considerable revenue by selling the patents for those improvements.[5] In 1876, Edison took that money and built a new complex for himself in the rural town of Menlo Park, New Jersey, a stop on the main line between New York City and Philadelphia. In its six years of operation, Menlo Park generated over four hundred patents and became known as the "invention factory." Over time, the popular image of Edison alone in his giant facility tinkering away on breakthrough innovations developed, despite the fact that it in no way resembled what actually happened in Menlo Park. Edison was no lone inventor, but rather he compiled a team of engineers, machinists, and physicists who worked together on many of the inventions we now attribute to Edison alone. The team referred to themselves as "muckers" and overtook the upstairs space of Edison's Menlo Park warehouse. There were approximately fourteen muckers working alongside Edison, including Charles Batchelor, John Adams, John Kruesi, John Ott, and Charles Wurth. Many of them have their names alongside or even in front of Edison's on the patents created at Menlo Park. It's worth noting that Edison's name alone sits atop the patent for "Improvement in Electric Lights." However, that patent was filed in 1878, two years after building his Menlo Park facility, so the likelihood that Edison worked entirely independently on the technology for this patent is small. Most of the further improvements in lightbulbs, telegraphs, and phonographs that we attribute to Edison were actually derived from or included the work of the muckers, while Edison spent a considerable amount of time dealing with clients, speaking to the press, or entertaining potential investors.

The team at Menlo Park worked on various projects, some for Edison's clients, some for clients of their own, and even some side projects just for fun. They worked closely together, often sharing the same workshop space despite being involved with separate projects. They shared machines, traded stories, and passed along insights or ideas they believed might be helpful for other projects or unknown future work. Their ideas and insights cross-pollinated; Edison and the muckers were unapologetic about borrowing ideas from clients in one industry and applying them to an invention in another field. In some cases, they borrowed ideas and even physical parts from other projects. If you walk through the reconstructed Menlo Park laboratory in Dearborn, Michigan (it was taken down, transported, and assembled into a museum by Henry Ford), you'll notice prototype machines with whole parts missing. These weren't lost in the moving or reconstruction of Menlo Park; they were stolen by muckers themselves and used on other projects. Muckers were notorious for taking parts right from other working machines if they felt that the need was great enough, and Menlo Park had a wide range of clients, which gave Edison and his muckers a lot to work with. The muckers at Menlo Park were such a fertile source of ideas that it seems odd that their presence is typically dropped from the story most often told. But this isn't a coincidence. It was by design.

As their worked progressed, the team of muckers quickly realized the power behind Edison's name. They found that when they advertised their ideas or tried to sell themselves to potential clients, their audience seemed to like the notion that a single individual had authorship of their ideas, especially when that person was Edison. In the ongoing struggle for new investors, many of the muckers found that the celebrity associated with Edison's name was too valuable to ignore. So they began turning Edison the man into Edison the mythological lone genius. Edison alone drew better publicity than Edison and the muckers. Even the popular story of Edison's "worldwide" search for the perfect filament likely began as a publicity campaign designed to draw attention to and generate interest in the lightbulb. In fact, Edison had already found the bamboo fibers in a folding fan lying in his workshop when the story began to circulate. To those outside Menlo Park, Edison was a lone genius responsible for an astonishing array of inventions. But according to Francis Jehl, Edison's long-time assistant, those inside knew that "Edison [was] in reality a collective noun and [meant] the work of many men."[6]

Edison's team took full advantage of the Lone Creator Myth that people want so much to believe in. For them, it was worth succumbing to the myth in order to find the funding needed to develop groundbreaking innovations. But this myth is promulgated in more than just the technological arena. It shows up in almost every creative field. In art, we hold an image of Michelangelo perched alone, high atop some scaffolding, laboring endlessly to paint the ceiling of the Sistine Chapel. In actuality, Michelangelo had assembled a team of thirteen artists to help complete the work.[7] In film, consider Academy Award–winning screenwriter Ron Bass. Bass relies on a team of six writers and researchers to help him draft storyboards and write scripts. This team approach has led Bass to write or cowrite sixteen feature films that earned a combined profit of over $2 billion. Those who cling to the Lone Creator Myth too strongly are apt to criticize Bass for his collaborative methods. To certain purists, even screenwriting should be a lonely endeavor. Like Edison, Michelangelo and Bass should be looked at not only as creators but also as entrepreneurs, creating a good-sized operation around the strength of their name and developing a stronger name because of their collaborative operation.

In 1995, Kevin Dunbar decided to research how collaboration happened in another field where the Lone Creator Myth dominates: science. Dunbar, a psychologist at McGill University, set up a rather unusual laboratory experiment that broke with the traditional methods of scientific inquiry used in psychology and instead emulated the field studies of anthropology and ethnography. Where traditional psychology research involves gathering a sample and administering surveys or tests, ethnography and anthropology research is more concerned with observing behaviors in the wild. In Dunbar's case, the "wild" was the research laboratories of microbiologists. Dunbar set up cameras inside four prominent microbiology laboratories in order to study where and how their breakthrough insights occurred.[8] Like art and inventing, science tends to hold tightly to the Lone Creator Myth, often attributing a team effort to the first named author on a research paper or the most famous name on the list. Dunbar's study, however, found that breakthrough insights usually don't occur alone in the lab the way we'd imagine. Instead, they happen most often at the conference table. Most of the important ideas generated by these four labs emerged not during experimentation but during the regular lab meetings where researchers would gather to share information and discuss setbacks or odd findings. As the scientists shared their findings, others in the team would notice connections to their own projects or the projects of scientists in their network. When the scientists shared their setbacks, the others on the team would also share problems from similar but slightly different research and also how they overcame those problems. From these connections, innovative solutions emerged. Interestingly, when Dunbar would follow up with many of the individual scientists, they wouldn't be able to accurately recall where their creative insight came from. They confabulated. Some appeared to have constructed their own stories. Few gave full credit to something as mundane as the lab meetings.

Dunbar also found that those labs with more diverse teams of individuals—people from different backgrounds and working on different projects—generated more creative insights and produced more significant research. Even in a field as advanced and specialized as microbiology, Dunbar's scientists operated in a similar fashion to Edison's muckers, working alongside each other and sharing diverse knowledge. What Dunbar's research didn't find, however, was just how diverse a team needed to be for optimal creativity. For that we have to move from the microbiology lab to the Broadway stage.

No Broadway production is the creation of just one person. Even so-called one-man shows require a crew of people to help with writing, staging, lighting, and everything that goes into taking a production from the initial idea to opening night. This need for collaboration is what drew the attention of two management professors, Brian Uzzi of Northwestern University and Jarrett Spiro of INSEAD. Uzzi and Spiro wanted to know how much the level of diversity and collaboration affected the creativity and success of a Broadway musical. Most of the artists on Broadway work on more than one musical at a time and thus develop relationships with members of the various

112

teams they are working on simultaneously. Sometimes the artists find themselves working with many of the same people on multiple different projects; other times each project brings almost solely new relationships. Uzzi and Spiro designed a study to examine if the strength or diversity of those relationships somehow affected the success or quality of the shows.

Together, Uzzi and Spiro analyzed almost every musical produced on Broadway from 1945 to 1989.[9] They even included shows that died in preproduction, as collaboration happened and connections were undoubtedly made. Collecting all this information was no easy feat. Some records were easily obtainable from previous research; other times, the team had to find the original playbills or magazine reviews to gather all the necessary data. "At the time, there wasn't an Internet database for Broadway," Spiro recounts. "We utilized these multiple sources to construct the full set of musicals and inputted the data manually. To fill the few remaining holes in the data, or to gather missing information about specific shows, we had to go through decades of the magazine *Variety* on microfilm."[10] The end result was a database of 474 musicals and 2,092 artists, including numerous Broadway legends from Cole Porter to Andrew Lloyd Webber. Once the database was built, the duo analyzed each show to calculate the complex network of collaborations and working relationships among producers, writers, actors, and choreographers. The research showed that the world of Broadway musicals was indeed a dense and interconnected web, with many individuals working together on a production, then going their separate ways, only to find themselves working with some of the same people years later on a new production. This dynamic produced for the Broadway community what is now called a "small-world network," a fertile ground for teams to connect, collaborate, disband, and repeat the cycle.

Uzzi and Spiro even found a way to measure the level of repeat collaborations in any given production year, a value they called the "small-world quotient" or simply Q. The Q score was a measurement of how diverse or homogenous the Broadway production teams were for that year. When Q was high, the teams were densely interconnected, which meant that more artists knew each other and were working together on multiple projects. When Q was low, there wasn't as much familiarity, and multiple collaborations were seldom. Uzzi and Spiro then compared each year's Q score to the level of financial success and critical acclaim achieved by the shows that year. Given what we know about teams, it would be logical to assume that those production crews with a higher Q, those teams who had lots of experience working together in the past, would perform better and would produce shows that were more creative and successful. Uzzi and Spiro's research found that this assumption held true, but, surprisingly, only to a certain point. Instead of a straight line indicating a rise in success as there was a rise in collaboration, the trend line looked more like an inverted U. "When I first saw the result, I thought, 'This is big,'" recalls Uzzi. "This was the first evidence using big data that showed that a community's network structure was related to the success of the creative artists within it."[11] As the Q of a production year went up, representing the diversity of the network structure, so did the year's financial and artistic successes, until a higher Q led to a decrease in the success measurements. Uzzi and Spiro calculated the optimal Q at around 2.6 on a scale of 1 to 5. With a Q score of 2.6, the chances of any given musical in that year being a hit were two-and-a-half times greater than the lowest-Q years, and the chances that the show would receive critical acclaim were three times greater.

Uzzi and Spiro's findings recognize the strength and fragility of team collaboration. The creativity of a production is enhanced when diverse people work together. In addition, the closeness of a team affects its performance, as total strangers forced to work together can have problems exchanging ideas. But people who are overly familiar with each other aren't that good for creativity either. In those cases, the artists are often so close and share such a common background that they all draw from the same material and fail to produce any truly new ideas—a kind of creative groupthink. Collaborations built from a combination of close connections and fresh perspectives enhance the likelihood of success, as individuals can quickly establish norms for collaboration but also benefit from the differing experiences and knowledge brought in by new artists. "The best teams for innovation are a blend of old colleagues and newbies because innovation only occurs when there is the introduction of new and/or novel ideas and a viable and well-developed output is produced from them," Spiro explains. "The newbies provide the novel ideas and the old colleagues provide the knowledge of how to work together to produce an output from those novel ideas that others will recognize as valuable."[12]

To accomplish the optimal blend of diversity on production teams, Broadway as a whole needs to build a network with just the right combination of new, diverse viewpoints and experienced colleagues. "The rotation of team personnel is critical to creativity," argues Uzzi. "Even if it comes at the loss of efficient communication among team members that have come to know each other and their work habits well."[13] This perfect blend would allow the artists to interact efficiently—because they would have communication processes established—but they would also benefit from incorporating new ideas.

Uzzi and Spiro's findings help explain the phenomenon in Dunbar's laboratories, where the more diverse teams yielded more creative insights and breakthroughs. If all the scientists were working on the same experiment and had the same backgrounds, they'd all think of the same potential explanations. However, in the laboratories running different experiments with people from different fields, everyone benefited from the knowledge of everyone else's past experiences. As scientists encountered setbacks or strange findings, it was the colleagues with different backgrounds who provided the best potential solutions. (It's worth mentioning that in Dunbar's case, the fact that these were microbiology labs in particular kept the groups from becoming too diverse.) In the case of Edison's muckers, the story is the same. Edison didn't just recruit friends from the telegraph industry. He hired a variety of engineers, machinists, and scientists. He created a network of muckers from diverse backgrounds from which to build diverse teams. In addition, the muckers didn't just collectively focus on one project at a time. Instead they were working on many projects simultaneously, with teams of people forming around a project as needed and disbanding when the project was complete so as to focus on something else. Edison's muckers had achieved an optimal blend of new perspectives and old experience.

Taken together, Dunbar's and Uzzi and Spiro's findings imply something that stands counter to the Lone Creator Myth: creativity is a team sport. Those teams operate best when they are a healthy mix of preexisting and new connections—shared experiences and totally new perspectives. Teams with a wide knowledge of creative ideas and an efficient means of sharing them are best suited to produce new, innovative work. If the most creative teams are built around this combination of old colleagues and new faces, then the most creative companies might be self-contained small-world networks. If an organization can build itself into a small-world network that allows the right blend of people to form teams as needed, then this perfect blend would allow collaborators to interact efficiently, and the company could enhance the likelihood of continued creative success.

When you think about places where creative networks can flourish and allow for such perfectly blended teams, certain cities come to mind: New York City, San Francisco, Paris. Few people think of Newton, Massachusetts. Yet that is where a relatively unknown partnership began building a design and innovation firm known as Continuum, which went on to have a huge impact in fields as diverse as consumer goods, financial services, athletic equipment, retail design, and even medical devices.[14] Since its founding in 1983, Continuum has grown from that small shop to a two-hundred-person organization with offices in cities across the globe, including Los Angeles, Seoul, Shanghai, and Milan. In less than thirty years, Continuum has won more than two hundred design awards, including more than seventy-five International Design Excellence Awards, and has designed groundbreaking products including medical instrumentation, new banking models, industrial robotics, the Reebok Pump, and even the Swiffer product line (including Dry, Wet Jet, and Duster).

Clients approach Continuum mostly for help with new product, service, or experience designs and improvements, but the stage of development those products or services are in varies widely. Some clients need research and early conceptual work, some require extended research leading to major strategy development, others need help solving technical problems that arise in their internal designs, and some need to develop a complex medical device or even a new business model. Often clients approach Continuum with one problem and leave with another. That's because the diverse perspectives brought by the team at Continuum allow them to step back and take a broader look at the client's needs. "When we first started, we began most of our projects at what we called Phase Zero," says Continuum founder Gianfranco Zaccai.[15] "Phase Zero was actually stepping back from what we were asked to design and understanding really what the context was of the product we were asked to innovate. The concept of Phase Zero grew into our strategy work, which is now the fundamental part of our business."

To achieve this level of innovation, Zaccai has brought together a diverse set of team members, including traditional designers, engineers, psychologists, artists, MBAs, and ethnographers. "The idea is that the design and innovation that we were doing was really a continuum that involves multiple disciplines collaborating together and leveraging the deep knowledge that our clients might have with the broad knowledge that we would bring to the party," says Zaccai. This diverse pool of talent assembles as needed around client projects, sometimes working on several projects at a time. Continuum is deliberate about securing clients from a variety of fields, so that designers are exposed to a diverse set of design and business challenges and can cross-pollinate ideas from different industries, life experiences, and cultural perspectives. A critical part of this team is the voice of the customer, which is gathered not from focus groups but rather from entering into the lives of regular human beings with ethnographic research.

Procter & Gamble's revolutionary Swiffer Wet Jet was created when P&G approached Continuum to create a new business around cleaning home floors, which might include a new cleaning tool. After lengthy research into the ways people clean floors in real-life situations, Continuum realized that many people spent as much time cleaning their mops as they did cleaning their floors and that a dirty mop just moved dirt around on the floor. It did little to remove the dirt. The company needed to develop a product that would speed up the cleaning process and make it, frankly, cleaner. Its new challenge wasn't to provide customers with simply a cleaner floor but to design a cleaner and quicker way to mop the floor. The team used that knowledge to design a new cleaning tool:

essentially a moistened towel on a stick that could be thrown away once it was soiled. It was a faster, or perhaps swifter, way to a clean floor.

Inside the teams at Continuum, multiple opinions and perspectives are shared during collaboration. Positions are formed and fought for. Arguments sometimes occur. Unlike in a lot of organizations, though, the "winning" argument isn't one person's perspective, but a result of the combined expertise of everyone in the room. During this process of combining perspectives, the common goal remains the same: to design an amazing experience for the end user that is also economically compelling for the client company. Continuum's designers believe that their experience and knowledge of the customer combined with the client's capabilities can bring about an innovative design that is truly of benefit to the world. This collaborative chaos may seem like a freeform brawl, but the process yields breakthrough innovations.

In 1988, Continuum was approached by Reebok to design a response to Nike's new Air technology, which integrated materials inside the heel of the shoe to capture and return an athlete's energy. Nike's innovation (and Michael Jordan's name) had catapulted Nike to success, and it soon surpassed Reebok as the leading producer of footwear in the United States. After some initial research, Continuum concluded that it wasn't possible to create a meaningful "energy return" system like what Nike claimed to have. "My cofounder, Jerry Zindler, is a trained physicist and was on our team for the project, and an analysis of the physics determined that it just didn't work beyond a minimal improvement," Zaccai recalls. "We developed and evaluated a bunch of ideas to provide an energy return system, but we realized that it didn't make any real difference in performance." Beyond that, it wouldn't be enough for Reebok to design a similar system. "It was kind of a 'me-too' solution," Zaccai confesses. In order to have an impact in the market, Reebok would need to invent something totally new. As part of the Continuum team's research, they observed a high school basketball team in action in order to identify the players' needs. They found fast-growing kids whose performance on the court was affected by shoes that were either too tight or too loose. They also found frustrated parents who couldn't afford to buy new shoes for their children every few months to keep up with their growth. At the same time, Zaccai recalls, a famous Boston Celtics player was sitting out most of the season with an ankle injury.

Fast-growing feet and an ankle injury might seem unrelated to most, but the combination helped Continuum generate totally new ideas. "We thought, 'What if we could stabilize the ankle? What if we could provide a really lightweight way of stabilizing the ankle that allowed you to play basketball closer to your full capability—and at the same time provide a custom fit to the kids on the corner just like the NBA players have when they have their shoes custom-made for them?'" While working on their new ideas, Zaccai remembered his past experience designing a conceptual project—an inflatable cast that used air to immobilize injuries and that allowed ski patrollers to stabilize a fallen skier's leg or arm while the skier was brought to first aid. The Continuum team realized that such an inflatable air pocket around the ankle of a shoe might help prevent injuries from happening without adding significant weight to the shoe. Some members of the team also had extensive experience in the health care environment, and they realized that IV bags are made with high reliability and low cost by welding two sheets of plastic together, and that such a design could be modified to create air bladders that could be inserted inside the new shoe to make their idea viable. Continuum also realized that inflating the shoe to the right pressure would have to be an individual choice, and that a convenient way of making that possible would be to integrate the bag into the shoe itself rather than designing a separate device. Continuum's engineers were able to create a component that could be inserted into the shoe during manufacturing. The Reebok Pump was born.

To the team at Reebok, the idea was revolutionary. To the team at Continuum, it seemed logical that their previous experiences and knowledge from different fields culminated in this new insight. Although any design team could have come up with the idea of an inflatable shoe, Continuum's process of combining different skill sets enabled them to quickly identify the right idea, conduct testing on a crude prototype to demonstrate its value, and then implement it quickly and cheaply. Collectively, the Continuum team had enough past experience to ferret out unmet consumer needs, build consensus within Reebok, and get these ideas into production and to the market. They used existing technologies and familiar suppliers to create a product that innovated Reebok's product line. The entire project cost less than $450,000 and brought Reebok over $1 billion in sales shortly after it was introduced to the market.

Continuum's innovation and Reebok's Pump shoe aren't the result of a single company's efforts, but of a collaboration between Continuum, Reebok, and a host of suppliers like the IV bag maker. Likewise, the Continuum team can't point to any one designer and attribute credit for the idea or the prototype. Instead, Continuum's system of collaboration deserves the credit. Continuum has created a company that functions as a network from which design teams form and reform as the needs of a particular project demand. Through its past work and its current designers, Continuum has built a network of relationships that consistently spark creative insights. "Every time we take on a new project, we craft a team based on what we think will uncover the most beneficial and useful information," Zaccai explains. "So we work closely with clients to understand what their issues are and then we put the right people in place." Just as in Spiro and Uzzi's Broadway productions, it was the combination of the diverse people from Continuum and from the client organization that made the new design of the Reebok Pump such a success.

Whether it's Edison's muckers, Dunbar's scientists, or a project team at Continuum, the right blend of diverse experience and efficient sharing of knowledge yields groundbreaking innovation. The Lone Creator Myth, however, can lead us to ignore these blended teams and give the credit to one individual. This myth can actually be harmful to our creativity. If we believe that innovation is a solo effort, then we're more likely to remove ourselves from the networks we need. We try to mimic the imagined starving poets, reclusive painters, or lonely inventors we've heard about, thinking that doing so will help us produce more great ideas. However, the most innovative companies in the world understand the need for diversity and make sure that project teams have a rotating cast of new and old members. The teams connect, collaborate, disband, and repeat. When individuals are given the chance to form teams around their diverse interests and their past experiences, the potential for creativity is enhanced. Continuum's most significant innovation isn't a new shoe or a different kind of floor mop. Instead, it's the process the company has uncovered for creating the right project teams and continuously tweaking them to blend fresh insights and shared experiences. Because of those teams, innovations like the Reebok Pump aren't standalone success stories for Continuum. Creative products like it are designed every day.

The Brainstorming Myth

When most organizations need to unleash creativity, they follow largely the same formula: assemble a team of people, put them in a room with whiteboard markers or sticky notes, and tell them to spit out as many ideas as they can. In short, they brainstorm. Or rather they engage in what they think is brainstorming. They believe in the *Brainstorming Myth*. The myth tells them that a great idea is all they need to produce innovation, and that by generating as many ideas as possible, they will find a single notion that they can bet their new project on. Once they get together and throw out ideas, they can sift through the pile and find that one, fully formed idea that's ready to display to the world. After that, they're done. Brainstorming becomes the beginning and the end of their creative process. It's quite telling that most books on creativity and innovation focus on this myth. The standard creativity book is filled with exercises for generating as many ideas as possible inside a short period of time. Rapid idea generation, whether done alone or in groups, gets reinforced as the essence of creativity. What makes the Brainstorming Myth so prevalent (and so dangerous) is that there is nothing inherently bad about brainstorming as a technique for generating ideas, and generating ideas is an important element of creativity. When done correctly, brain-storming helps teams assemble a pool of ideas from which they can pick the most novel and useful. But it's rarely done cor-rectly. And sometimes it doesn't need to be done at all.

In the mid-1980s, the beer industry was anything but creative. It was dominated by three big brewers, Anheuser-Busch, Coors, and Miller, who were able to keep competition to a minimum by either acquiring smaller upstarts or mimicking their products and using their own massive distribution networks to drive the upstarts out of business. If consumers wanted to drink something different at the time, they had to look to imports from other countries. The American market consisted almost entirely of light lagers that many people felt tasted the same; the only substantial choice offered was the label on the bottle.

So in 1984, when Jim Koch decided to become the sixth generation of Koch men to enter the beer industry, his father was anything but pleased. Koch holds three degrees from Harvard and had a successful career with the Boston Consult-ing Group before he decided to give it up to pursue brewing. "I had told my dad I wanted to leave my job and continue this 150-year-old family tradition and I'd thought we were going to have a warm, father-son moment," Koch recalls.[1] "He just looked at me and said, 'You've done some dumb things in your life, but this is just about the dumbest.'"

Because of his education and business experience, Koch knew that if he was going to compete, he needed to differentiate his brewery from the big three by offering something truly different. This is where most people would go to work coming up with ideas for products and potential marketing campaigns. Before betting on a strategy, they would generate as many potential products as possible and experiment to see which ones the market favored. Koch took a little different approach: he went out for a drink.

Before his unexpectedly poor father-son moment, while Koch was still toying with the idea of starting a brewery of his own, he found himself in a local pub. After taking a stool and settling into his surroundings, he noticed a man close to him drinking a Heineken, an expensive beer imported from Holland.[2] Koch asked him why he'd chosen that specific beer. "I like imported beer," the man answered. Koch asked him how he found the taste. "It tastes skunky," the man replied, a shocking confession given the man's previously stated preference for imports. *Skunky* is an industry term for the taste of spoiled beer. Beer has a shelf life, just like any other food, and exposure to light drastically reduces that shelf life. The more light, the quicker it spoils and the more it tastes skunky. Imported beer has to travel long distances and is often shipped in clear or green bottles, which filter out less light than the traditional brown bottles. While talking to this man in the pub, Koch had his creative idea. Instead of competing with the big three brewers, which many had tried and failed to do, he could compete in the higher-end import market with a much fresher tasting beer. "Their whole business model was based on selling stale and skunky beer to Americans and trying to cover it up with this old-world imagery," Koch says. After a short conversation with a total stranger, Koch had his positioning down. He just needed a high-end beer with old-world imagery.

Instead of creating a lab and testing multiple recipes, Koch went to his father's house. "We went up to the attic and got out my great-grandfather's recipe, Louis Koch Lager, and he said, 'This is really good beer,' " Koch recalls. "I took the recipe home and made it in my kitchen as best I could. When it was finished aging and I tasted it, I knew I had something." Koch's ancestral recipe would eventually become Samuel Adams Boston Lager, the flagship brew of Koch's Boston Beer Company. There was still a lot of work Jim Koch would need to do to make his old family recipe the centerpiece of a thriving beer company. He had to develop the product and create a market niche, which involved educating consumers on the basics of beer production and how his product stood out. Because of his initial idea, however, the Boston Beer Company has become the largest craft brewery in the United States.

Although Koch's beers represent only around 1 percent of the total beer market in the United States, his company's impact has gone far beyond that. Many believe that Koch single-handedly started the U.S. craft brewing revolution. Today, there are roughly fifteen hundred craft breweries in the United States that bring to market a wide array of creative brews, infused with such ingredients as cocoa, berries, coffee, and even tree seeds.[3] "I want American craft brewing and American beer culture to be recognized all over the world as the epitome of the brewer's art," Koch says. "I want the rest of the world to look at America and go, 'That's where the best beers in the world come from.' It happens to be true today, and we have to keep doing it and innovating in order for the realization to take hold in the rest of the world."[4] The Boston Beer Company has positioned itself to lead that change, having released over forty different types of beer in the company's nearly thirty-year history, including seasonals and collaborations with breweries across the globe.

With so much creativity at Boston Beer Company and in the beer industry today, it's hard to believe that the initial spark for all of this came from a simple conversation at a bar and an old family recipe. "To me, the ideas come from real-world stimulation," Koch says. And he finds ideas everywhere, from the wholesalers he meets with to the retailers and bars he visits to check in on his product.[5] Koch's method runs counter to the Brainstorming Myth many people believe, that if you want to have creative ideas, you simply have to generate a lot of ideas.

It's likely that the Boston Beer Company benefits from brainstorming sessions when it considers new marketing initiatives or even new recipes. However, its primary product, and much of its success, came about without this particular technique for rapid idea generation. Nobel laureate (two times over) Linus Pauling was correct when he said, "The best way to get good ideas is to get lots of ideas."[6] But the trouble with brainstorming and the reason for the perpetuation of the Brainstorming Myth is twofold: (1) brainstorming is conducted as a lone event for idea generation, and (2) brainstorming isn't done properly.

Brainstorming, or rapid idea generation, is a useful technique for leveraging the creativity of a group to produce novel ideas. Recall, however, that creativity isn't just about novel ideas. Those ideas must also be useful in order to be truly creative. To make sure they are useful, you need to do more than just brainstorm. "When most organizations do brainstorming, it isn't very effective," says R. Keith Sawyer.[7] Sawyer is one of the most prominent researchers on creativity and collaboration. A professor of education, psychology, and business at Washington University in St. Louis, Sawyer has studied the creative process for decades and did his doctoral studies under Mihaly Csikszentmihalyi. Recall from Chapter Two that Csikszentmihalyi's research puts forth that the creative process has five stages. Sawyer's work built upon his doctoral mentor's by combining it with a broader review of other research-based attempts to construct a model of the creative process. For Sawyer this meant not just conducting interviews but also reading a lot of research and trying to synthesize it all into one cohesive process.

When he had processed all of the available research, Sawyer concluded that as individuals and teams seek to produce creative work, their output comes as a result of moving through eight distinct stages:[8]

1. *Find and define the problem.* Creativity often comes when you identify a good problem or ask a question in a novel way or formulate a challenge in just the right way to lead down a surprising path.

2. *Gather relevant knowledge.* Generating and evaluating novel and useful ideas require a substantial amount of knowledge about the domain.

3. *Gather potentially related information.* Knowledge of the domain is vital, but sometimes the best solutions also involve ideas and concepts from outside the given domain.

4. *Take time off for incubation.* As discussed in Chapter Two, the unconscious mind needs time to process and associate all the information in new ways.

5. *Generate a large variety of ideas.* After incubation, ideas and connections are brought back to the surface so that the conscious mind can give them proper attention.

6. *Combine ideas in unexpected ways.* As discussed in Chapter Four, many creative ideas are the result of new combinations of existing ideas or inventions.

7. *Select the best ideas.* Generating novel ideas is wonderful, but effective creators must be able to identify which ones are also useful in order to pursue those further.

8. *Externalize the idea.* Creativity is never a complete process; ideas develop, transform, and evolve as they interact with the outside world.

Sawyer's eight-stage creative process doesn't replace brainstorming. Instead, Sawyer recognizes the potential of brainstorming when used inside the larger process of bringing creative ideas to the world. When done properly, brainstorming can become part of stage five, generating lots of ideas. In this way, it is a technique for divergent thinking, but it also must be paired with convergent thinking in order to move toward the best possible idea. Convergent thinking occurs as ideas are combined and evaluated (stages six and seven). Equally important to both divergent and convergent thinking is the information gathering that occurs before brainstorming ever takes place (stages two and three). Without the right knowledge, it's difficult to generate the right ideas and difficult to evaluate which ideas have the most potential. Taken as a stage in Sawyer's larger creative process, brainstorming becomes one of the best tools for generating new and useful ideas. As mentioned previously, however, brainstorming in practice is rarely done effectively. Most people equate brainstorming with getting a crowd together and throwing out potential ideas. After a few ideas are tossed around, the loudest person in the room or the one with the highest rank usually forces consensus around his original idea. This is not only contrary to Sawyer's larger creative process; it's actually counter to the method prescribed by brainstorming's original creator, Alex Osborn.

Indeed, brainstorming has been so abused and misused that it's difficult to think of it as having an original developer. However, the process of brainstorming was originally developed by Osborn in 1957.[9] Osborn was a founding partner at the renowned advertising firm BBDO and author of *Applied Imagination*, one of the first books on creativity in business. Osborn's book was an attempt to codify the creative process that he and his team used at BBDO. It is in *Applied Imagination* that Osborn first coined the term "brainstorming." He researched the environment that his advertising teams collaborated in and found that their creativity was most stimulated when certain "rules" were followed:[10]

1. Generate as many ideas as possible.
2. Defer judgment on all ideas.

3.   Generate wild ideas.

4.   Build upon each other's ideas.

Osborn believed that by following these rules, teams would experience a drastic increase in their creative output compared to their standard practice of getting together to "throw out some ideas." It turns out he was correct. Research has shown that properly run brainstorming sessions, especially when run by a trained facilitator, produce more and better-quality ideas than freestyle collaboration.[11] Brainstorming works, but it doesn't work alone.

Even Osborn recognized that gathering people in a room and merely brainstorming was insufficient for producing truly creative ideas. To him, creative ideas and solutions involved spending time considering three things: facts, ideas, and solutions.[12] Osborn believed that creative teams needed to spend sufficient time with each of these components individually. Instead of jumping right to solutions, which many would-be brainstormers do, teams should have ample time to discuss the facts and information surrounding whatever it is that needs to be done. Only then can the process of generating and evaluating ideas be undertaken. In effect, Osborn created a three-stage process of fact finding, idea generating, and solution evaluating that resembles Sawyer's larger eight-stage process.

In addition, when most people brainstorm, they focus too much on ideas as individual entities, not as building blocks for more ideas. "A lot of people view brainstorming in an additive way—we're adding to the number of ideas," Sawyer explains. "But that's not the power of the group. The group's power comes from the synergy that goes beyond the additive. What the most creative companies do is tell the members of the group to come up with lists of ideas *before* they come to the brainstorming session. What the group is really powerful for is exchanging ideas and then having ideas bump up against one another and merge in surprising new ways that any one person might not have thought of on their own." As ideas combine and transform, they add to the total number of ideas generated, but the new ideas are also drastically higher in quality. This is the practice Sawyer describes in his stage six: combine ideas in unexpected ways.

Creativity isn't just about idea generation. This is why Sawyer's last stage—externalizing the idea—is so important:. "I think most people don't realize how important externalizing your ideas is," Sawyer argues. "Ideas don't appear in your head fully formed. You have a glimmer and then you start working on it. Then, in the process of working, you notice something else. Then you may go in a different direction. It ends up feeling very improvisational, and the improvisation comes from the creator interacting with some external representation of what they're thinking." This improvisation allows ideas to be combined, and it leads to new, potentially better ideas. It's a vital stage for teams trying to produce a high-quality end result.

For Sawyer, the important element to remember isn't how to brainstorm—or how to use any other technique to generate ideas, for that matter. It's that all eight stages are respected and integrated. To emphasize this, Sawyer even shies away from labeling his own process as a series of stages. "I think of them primarily as practices or disciplines, not even really as stages," Sawyer says. "They alternate. You go through all of them. You use them at different times of the day. And they tend to roughly fall in a chronological sequence, but a lot of times they don't." As any outstandingly creative person or team knows, creativity is never a perfectly linear process. Sawyer uses his final stage, externalizing, as an example. "I say it's the final stage in the sequence, but clearly it's there from the beginning. You should start externalizing ideas right at the beginning, and that gives you new ideas; it changes the way you think about the problem." In Sawyer's well-researched view, the externalization of an idea should happen at each stage so that the ideas are constantly improving. It's even what makes proper brainstorming so effective. Sessions are opportunities to externalize ideas and allow them to transform.

Elements of these individual stages can also be seen in the story of Jim Koch and his creation of Samuel Adams Boston Lager. Although Koch didn't use a brainstorming session to generate recipes for his brew, his extensive research and knowledge of the beer market allowed him to properly evaluate his family's recipe and understand how to position it to the public. Koch's mental process largely followed Sawyer's eight steps. He was born into a family of brewers, which gave him insight into the problem and relevant knowledge. Following his fateful trip to the bar, the idea for competing with imported beer was the insight at the end of a time of incubation. In moving from idea to final product, Koch had to evaluate his idea and externalize it through testing and, ultimately, the product launch. Had Koch run a brainstorming session around the idea, it's unlikely that he'd have stumbled upon Samuel Adams and the strategy of competing against the high-end import market. "Your typical creativity advice book tells you how to have more ideas," says Sawyer. "That's jumping too far ahead. If you do everything else right, the ideas will just follow naturally. But if you try and have ideas without doing the other stuff, it's not going to happen. It's like waiting for corn to grow without planting any seeds." Koch's family history, his knowledge of the market, and his propensity to look for ideas from a variety of sources created a fertile ground in which the seeds of his future Samuel Adams Boston Lager were planted.

The story of Jim Koch and Samuel Adams isn't unique. When examining some of the most creative firms in the world, it's easy to see that they have moved beyond simple brainstorming and, in some cases, developed their own large-scale process for consistently producing novel and useful ideas. Their process isn't to rely on brainstorming alone. Instead, they engage in a series of practices and disciplines like those in Sawyer's eight stages, which ensures that their great ideas flow continuously. Consider one such design company, known simply as IDEO, that never seems to run out of great ideas.

Walking through the Palo Alto offices of the design firm IDEO, it's difficult to envision the company as a powerhouse consulting firm for Fortune 500 clients. Instead of the windowed offices and cubicle farms of many top consulting firms, IDEO's interior looks as scattered as the aftermath of a brainstorming session. There are bicycles hanging from the ceiling. The desks are decorated with a seemingly haphazard motif. There is even an airplane wing jutting out of one wall. With such a chaotic workspace, it's difficult to envision the company actually functioning. However, IDEO is perhaps one of the most consistently successful design firms in the world, and that success has led everyone from old-guard Fortune 500 companies to bold new start-ups to seek it out for help being more creative. In its just over two decades of existence, IDEO has designed more than four thousand products for nearly a thousand different clients and over fifty different industries—everything from medical devices to toothpaste dispensers. It has won more International Design Excellence Awards than any other firm.[13] *Fast Company* magazine called it "the world's most celebrated design firm" while also listing it as one of the twenty-five most innovative companies. It has even been ranked near the top of *Fortune*'s list of most desirable workplaces for MBA graduates—hard to believe for a firm that started out with rented space above a dress shop.

IDEO owes its success to a process it calls "design thinking."[14] This method has five steps: understand the market, observe, visualize, evaluate and refine, and implement. "Design thinking is a human-centered approach to innovation that draws from the designer's toolkit to integrate the needs of people, the possibilities of technology, and the requirements for business success," says Tim Brown, the current CEO of the company.[15] At first, the company was using this method to design tangible products, such the computer mouse, the PDA, and the pump dispenser for toothpaste. But as the design thinking method caught on and produced consistently innovative products, the company began dabbling in designing more than just objects, even going into experience design, such as reworking the blood donation experience for the American Red Cross.[16]

Before beginning to generate any ideas, IDEO designers dedicate a significant portion of time to research. They examine existing products in the market. They study the client organization and its customer base. They dig deep into the technologies being used and others that might be relevant. They even compile lists of their perceived constraints, although these may end up not being true constraints at all.

When the initial research is over, it's still not time to gather together and start listing ideas. Instead, the team takes to the field and observes real people using the existing products on the market or rough prototypes of new product designs. They note what comes easily and what confuses people, as well as people's likes and dislikes about the product. They study what needs are being met, what needs are not, and even whether the product itself creates any new needs. This commitment to observation is so intense that IDEO hires university-trained ethnographers to help them study how people interact with the current products.

Only after the market research and ethnographic studies have been completed is it time to generate ideas. IDEO largely relies on brainstorming to do this. "Brainstorming is the idea engine of IDEO," writes Tom Kelley, general manager at IDEO. "It's an opportunity for teams to 'blue sky' ideas early in a project or to solve a tricky problem that's cropped up later on. The more productive the group, the more it brainstorms regularly and effectively."[17] The design teams at IDEO adhere to a specific method for brainstorming; they don't just get in a room and throw out ideas.[18] Every session is led by a trained facilitator. The walls of most conference rooms are even painted with the rules for brainstorming, including "Encourage Wild Ideas" and "Go For Quantity." Even after generating ideas, however, the teams don't usually begin evaluating right away. Instead, they prototype, another vital element of their overall process. They use these prototypes to visualize their new concepts and imagine how customers will use them. These prototypes work best when they are three-dimensional models instead of pictures or drawings. It's too easy to dismiss a drawing outright, but people will interact with a model, and that can trigger surprising insights.

With several prototypes built, the team then evaluates each one. They get feedback from other designers, the client team, subject-matter experts, and even the target users. As they receive feedback, they continuously modify and combine prototypes to improve incrementally. "We try not to get too attached to the first few prototypes, because we know they'll change," writes Kelley. "No idea is so good that it can't be improved upon, and we plan on a *series* of improvements."[19] The design teams at IDEO know that as others interact with their products, the designers will gain a better understanding of which features work and which need improvement. From there, they can create even better iterations of the product.

Once this process is done and the final prototype is settled on, IDEO ships the final design to the client organization. Moving from the prototyped unit to an implementable product can be a long process, however. IDEO's prototype for the computer mouse, for example, was originally constructed using a rubber ball placed inside the lid from a butter dish.[20] It took a long time to transform such a low-fi object into a high-fi product, but IDEO's ability to solve the technical challenges without sacrificing elements of design is perhaps what makes it the world's leading design firm.

The design thinking method used by IDEO isn't anything new or proprietary. The steps in Kelley's outline closely resemble Sawyer's eight-stage creative process and Osborn's original three stages. All three processes assert that adequate research must be done before generating ideas. All three processes recognize that ideas change and improve as they are given more exposure. And all three processes include brainstorming and idea generation as a specific and vital stage. Most important, perhaps, all three place that idea generation stage inside a larger framework which ensures that the best ideas rise to the top. Although IDEO teams might be better at brainstorming than most organizations, it isn't this skill that pushes them creatively. Instead, it's their commitment to the entire creative process that gives them the ability to consistently produce outstanding creative products and design remarkable user experiences.

The Brainstorming Myth makes it easy to assume that the secret to producing innovation is simply to generate as many ideas as possible. As a practice, brainstorming is the most utilized technique in organizations (even if it's mostly utilized wrongly). However, the creative process is much more complex than simple idea generation. There is research to be done, prototypes to create, and new combinations of ideas to develop. The most innovative organizations don't rely on just one technique for generating ideas. Keith Sawyer argues that "brainstorming has to be embedded in a broader, longer-term organizational strategy where idea generation and creativity is a part of what goes on in the organization." It's this long-term strategy and a culture embedded with creativity and innovation that help companies like IDEO churn out good idea after good idea.

The Cohesive Myth

When you imagine the inner workings of any consistently creative team, you envision certain elements that seem to be requirements. You picture open floor plans, relaxed dress codes, pool tables, free food, and smiling, happy people everywhere. If you picture their collaboration, you imagine those teams being as happy creating as they are when playing pool. You picture teams that get along throughout the process. We assume that creative people thrive in fun, playful atmospheres and that they must therefore need playful interactions. This is the *Cohesive Myth*—the notion that the most creative ideas and products come from teams that suspend criticism and focus on consensus. The Cohesive Myth leads us to focus on team building, on making sure every person on the team works smoothly with everyone else. An excessive focus on cohesiveness, however, can actually dampen a team's creativity. It can narrow down options and cause those with a unique perspective to censor themselves rather than risk not being seen as part of the team. This myth is prevalent within a lot of organizations, but often the most creative teams, and most innovative companies, aren't focused on getting along all the time. While the exterior of these teams might seem as pleasant as we envisioned, their inner workings can sometimes pull creative insight from the opposite of cohesiveness: conflict.

The headquarters of Pixar Animation Studios, for example, make it look like the happiest and most cohesive place to work in the world. The company's sixteen-acre campus in Emeryville, California, has won architectural awards and has been featured in magazines and books for the beauty and intelligence of its design. When entering through the main doors, you're struck first by the sheer size of the atrium. The football field–sized room is a blend of glass windows, exposed brick, and riveted steel beams. The atrium's ceiling, two stories tall, is vaulted glass and steel, with bridges across the vast expanse and walkways along the walls of the second story. The atrium itself serves as the central hub for the entire building. It is home to the mailboxes, the café, the main bathrooms, and even a six-hundred-seat theater. Conference rooms line the side walls of the atrium, with glass, garage-door-style retractable walls for when the rooms aren't in use. The beauty of the campus shouldn't come as a surprise, given that the man who obsessed over the design and construction of the campus was Steve Jobs.

Pixar got its start not as a movie studio but as a computer hardware company. The roots of the company can be traced back to when George Lucas hired a team of computer animators (though that term was hardly used at the time) in the

1980s as part of a new computer division within Lucasfilm, though the relationships go back further. Lucas was interested in using computers to enhance cinematic special effects, or at least make them cheaper to produce. The idea that a computer could be used to make an entire feature film hadn't yet occurred to Lucas, but it had occurred to those he had hired. At the helm of this division was the trio of Ed Catmull, Alvy Ray Smith, and John Lasseter, all of whom were bent on using computers not just for special effects but to produce an entire movie. They even created a few short films to demonstrate their skills.

Despite their enthusiasm for making a feature film, Lucas only utilized the team once for the brief animation of a distant planet in *Star Trek II: The Wrath of Kahn*. Lucas, going through a costly divorce and tired of funding the expensive computer hardware, eventually soured on the idea of owning a computer division and sold the entire unit to Steve Jobs for $5 million (plus another $5 million in capital investments). Jobs was interested more in selling the hardware Pixar could design than in the short films Catmull, Smith, and Lasseter kept pushing to produce. However, he saw these films as an opportunity to demonstrate the power of Pixar's machines, so he kept funding them. Eventually, *Tin Toy*—a short film directed by Lasseter about a small metal toy trying to escape the destructive path of a young baby—achieved critical success and even won an Oscar. The success put Pixar in talks with the Walt Disney Company, who distributed Pixar's first full-length feature film, *Toy Story*.

Toy Story's breakthrough success began a hot streak of blockbuster feature films that continues to this day. The success of its sequel, *Toy Story 2*, funded the inspirational corporate campus envisioned by Steve Jobs. Jobs hired architect Peter Bohlin (who had also helped Jobs design the Apple Stores), and the two collaborated on a movie studio built like no other. Traditionally, movie studios sprawl out as wide as their campuses will allow, with separate buildings for each major function. Instead, Jobs wanted one building to house all employees. Jobs's theory was that a design scheme that steered employees toward a large central hub would result in large-scale collaboration. Jobs firmly believed that collaboration fueled the outstanding creative work Pixar sought and that chance encounters were the fuel for collaboration. The atrium is so large precisely because it is designed to be the home for these chance encounters. The mailboxes, bathrooms, game room, and conference rooms are all centrally located to force individuals from different divisions, with offices in different locations, to interact, share their work, and benefit from those discussions. The building was designed around Jobs's theory that chance encounters would prove to be serendipitous and help fuel collaboration and enhance quality. "Steve's theory worked from day one," Lasseter later recalled to Jobs's biographer.[1] "I kept running into people I hadn't seen for months. I've never been in a building that promoted collaboration and creativity as well as this one."

The Pixar team's collaborative creativity isn't just evidenced in their films; it can be seen in how they've transformed all areas of the Pixar headquarters. There are larger-than-life representations of Pixar characters scattered around the campus, including a gigantic replica of the company's signature character, Luxo Jr., an animated lamp from one of Pixar's first short films, just outside the building. Many of the individual offices have been arranged in a U shape, with a central gathering area in the middle that encourages unplanned discussions on a smaller scale than those in the grand atrium. Some of the individual offices aren't traditional offices at all. Instead, they resemble playhouses or tiki huts, whatever the offices' owners choose as a theme. Perhaps the most creative of all these examples is the Lucky 7 Lounge, a speakeasy hidden behind the bookcase of an animator's otherwise nondescript office. The lounge wasn't part of Jobs's original plan. Instead, it was created after animator Andrew Gordon's chance discovery of a small access door on the back wall of his office that led to a low corridor meant to provide access to the heating and air conditioning units. The animator and his colleagues transformed the bonus space with mood lighting, a full bar, and even custom-printed napkins.

From the eccentric offices to the smiling employees playing foosball or Ping-Pong, it's easy to see that the Pixar team members enjoy being around each other and collaborating on projects of all sizes, whether award-winning movies or hidden cocktail lounges. There is an energy to the campus that is felt around the atrium and in the chatter of employees all over the main building, now named the Steve Jobs Building in honor of its creator. It's impossible to resist extracting lessons about creative work teams and collaboration after seeing the Pixar campus. Pixar employees work together; they have fun together. Walking around the campus, it's hard to imagine employees fighting. Yet fight they do. For many of the animators at Pixar, conflict and debate are just part of their morning routine. It may be the happiest place to work in the world, but during these debates it can seem far from the most cohesive.

The animators, directors, and computer scientists at Pixar start many of their workdays inside a small screening room just off the main atrium where project teams gather for meetings, known as "dailies," to review their work from the previous day.[2] Those inside the screening room are given free rein to criticize and challenge every aspect of the animated frame. Nothing is left unexamined. No detail is too small to critique, and no one is prohibited from challenging someone else's work. Everything from the angle of the lighting to the timing of certain sound effects is brought up, discussed, and debated. Frame by frame, the Pixar team fights over the details before settling on how to improve the frame. Beyond just the dailies, Pixar filmmakers also attend quarterly meetings to review their work. "They present 'the film' to other filmmakers," explains Pixar president Ed Catmull, "and they'll go through and they will tear the film apart."[3] Given that it takes twenty-four animated frames to complete a second of movie footage, this can be a laborious process. But while "shredding" each frame can be draining, the Pixar teams know that the process is vital to their ability to release quality films again and again. The more debate around each frame, the higher the end quality of the film.

Pixar values friction so much that it is built into how teams are formed. After the success of *Finding Nemo*, Pixar's leadership worried that their company might be getting a little too comfortable with its creative process. They brought in director

Brad Bird as a member of the team. Before joining Pixar, Bird had worked with Warner Brothers on *The Iron Giant*, a traditional animation film that won critical acclaim but was also a failure at the box office. Pixar executives wanted Bird's first project with them to be different from their usual film offerings. They wanted to use Bird's entrance to create some productive friction at Pixar. "So I said, 'Give us the black sheep,'" Bird recalls. "'I want artists who are frustrated. I want the ones who have another way of doing things that nobody's listening to.'"[4] Bird recruited a team of malcontents for a new film that most believed couldn't be created inside the budget and technology constraints that existed. Bird's black sheep brought considerable friction to the process of making films, but it paid off. Pixar's *The Incredibles* was an instant hit at the box office and added two more Academy Awards to the company's trophy case. "We gave the black sheep a chance to prove their theories, and changed the way a number of things are done around here," Bird says. "For less money per minute than was spent on the previous film, *Finding Nemo*, we did a movie that had three times the number of sets and had everything that was hard to do."

It's easy to look at Pixar, or any creative team, and see its cohesiveness and friendly workplace as the reason for its success. From that perspective, the morning shredding sessions and hiring of malcontents may seem counterintuitive to the creative process and like a drastic contrast from the open, laid-back feeling of Pixar's main atrium. But just below the surface of many outstanding creative teams, you'll find that their process relies on structured conflict, not cohesion.

It's difficult to trace the Cohesive Myth back to its origins, but most cite brainstorming's creator Alex Osborn with popularizing the myth. Recall from Chapter Eight that Osborn's brainstorming is much more rigid than what most people have probably experienced. In *Applied Imagination*, Osborn wrote guidelines for facilitators and specific rules that must be observed for a brainstorming session to yield maximum creativity.[5] Chief among these rules is the idea of suspending criticism. It was Osborn's belief that criticism and conflict stifled creativity by triggering people to withhold their ideas for fear of criticism. So in order to get a team to generate large quantities of great ideas, he believed that teams needed everyone to share his or her ideas in a stream-of-consciousness fashion, holding nothing back from the group. If people withheld their ideas, then the entire brainstorming process would be subverted.

Although it most certainly existed before him, after the publication of Osborn's book, the pursuit of cohesiveness in creative teams truly began. Leagues of creativity theorists tried to validate his theories by conducting studies and building models in support of harmony and cohesion. Some of these theorists supported ideas similar to Osborn's concept of evaluation apprehension. Others believed that creative ideas developed deep inside the human brain, claiming that as we get older and more "sophisticated," our more advanced thought processes self-monitor our creative ideas and eliminate them in the presence of criticism and conflict. This theory appears to explain why children, uninhibited by self-monitoring, appear to be inherently creative, yet as they grow older and their actions are evaluated, most of them lose interest in creative pursuits. Logically then, if we want to recapture our creative thought process, we need to build an environment that emphasizes harmony, suspends judgment, and prevents conflict, the assumption being that such an environment would allow individuals to cease their self-monitoring and tap into their childlike creative process. However, a growing body of research supports the opposite conclusion. It could be that the conflict, evaluation, and confrontation brought about by expressing and debating differing viewpoints drive teams to an overall more creative output.

Perhaps the most famous study in support of the idea that conflict enhances creativity is an experiment that was led by Charlan Nemeth, a professor of psychology at the University of California, Berkeley. Nemeth and her team wanted to explore the role of conflict in generating and producing creative ideas.[6] They assembled participants into three separate experimental conditions (minimal, brainstorming, and debate) and formed them into teams within those conditions. Each team was tasked with generating ideas for the same challenge: how to reduce traffic congestion in the San Francisco Bay Area. The "minimal" teams were given no further instructions and told to develop as many ideas as possible. The "brainstorming" teams were given the traditional set of brainstorming rules: generate as many ideas as possible, defer judgment on all ideas, generate wild ideas, and build upon each other's ideas. Paramount among those rules was the notion that all judgment should be suspended and no idea criticized or debated. The "debate" teams were given a set of rules similar to the brainstorming teams but with one important difference. Instead of deferring judgment, they were told to debate and criticize others' ideas as they were generated.

When the results were calculated, the winners were clear. Although teams in the brainstorming condition did generate more ideas than the teams given minimal instructions, it was the teams in the debate condition that outperformed the rest, producing an average of 25 percent more ideas than the other two conditions in the same period of time. Even after the teams had disbanded, the influence of debate on the generation of ideas continued. In follow-up interviews with each subject, researchers asked the participants if they had any more ideas for solving the traffic problem. Each participant from the minimal and brainstorming conditions did have one or two more ideas, but participants in the debate condition gave an average of seven additional ideas per person.

Nemeth and her team considered that the study might have been a fluke or even a decidedly American phenomenon. To rule out these possibilities, they reran the experiment in Paris using the exact same methods and instructions, except that teams were asked to resolve the traffic problem for Paris, not San Francisco. The results were the same. Teams that utilized conflict in their process consistently outperformed teams that focused on cohesion. In a summary of the study's results, Nemeth challenges the conventional wisdom of suppressing debate: "Our findings show that it does not inhibit ideas but, rather, stimulate them relative to every other condition."[7]

Conflict and criticism aren't just useful for generating ideas. They may even be useful for elaborating on individual

150

ideas and weaving them together into a comprehensive whole. In a 1981 study conducted by Nancy Lowry and David Johnson, both psychologists at the University of Minnesota at the time, groups of fifth- and sixth-grade elementary schoolchildren were separated into teams and tasked with researching and writing a group report.[8] Half the teams were told to work together but to avoid conflict and compromise when agreement wasn't possible. The other half were instructed to listen to everyone's ideas but to be critical of the ones they didn't agree with. In the end, the students who were instructed to fight over their ideas produced a report with more in-depth research and a more logical presentation of the rationale behind their own ideas. They also displayed a greater ability to weave the ideas of many students together so that the end result was stronger and more comprehensive, showing that even at an early age, individuals are able to learn how to use constructive conflict when working together and allow that conflict to create a better end product.

The power of debate for improving the end result is something Alfred Sloan discovered on his own. The long-time chairman and CEO of General Motors once interjected during an important meeting by asking, "Gentlemen, I take it we are all in complete agreement on the decision here?"[9] Sloan then waited as each member of the assembled committee nodded in agreement. Sloan continued, "Then, I propose we postpone further discussion of this matter until our next meeting to give ourselves time to develop disagreement and perhaps gain some understanding of what this decision is about." Sloan knew that his team stood little chance of developing creative solutions to their problems unless he allowed for, and encouraged, disagreement.

The rationale behind Sloan's actions is supported by empirical research which shows that when ideas aren't yet fully formed, criticism and constructive conflict are vital to testing and strengthening the value of those ideas. "Constant argument can mean there is a competition to develop and test as many ideas as possible, that there is wide variation in knowledge and perspectives," explains Robert Sutton, professor of management science at Stanford University.[10] Conflict is an indicator that diverse viewpoints are being considered and that the competition for ideas is still ongoing. During this competition, ideas are strengthened through further research, longer consideration, or the blending of different ideas into one that is stronger. In contrast, when everyone in a group always agrees, it can indicate that the group doesn't have very many ideas, or that they value agreement more than quality suggestions. When teams always agree, they don't push their ideas as far as they can; so overly cohesive teams rarely produce outstandingly creative works, whereas teams that seek to improve their ideas through debate are far more likely to generate innovative ideas.

But fighting for the sake of fighting isn't likely to prove very effective either. It has to be the right kind of fight, and it has to be over something worth fighting for. There are two types of conflict: "interpersonal" or "emotional" conflict and "task" or "intellectual" conflict. In interpersonal conflict, people don't fight over the merits of the ideas; they fight over personal conflicts, power struggles, or even just a general dislike for each other. Rather than pushing ideas to become better, these conflicts are often toxic and can be destructive to individuals and teams. Task conflict, however, is notably more productive because it is limited to the facts and merits around an idea. People fight over which ideas are best, based not on their personal opinions but on the value of each suggestion. Feelings are spared because the structure of the fight keeps it focused on producing a better end result, not just winning or losing. However, limiting the conflict within a debate to task conflict alone is difficult. Groups that debate can often find that their arguments get personal. Conflict is good, but keeping that conflict good isn't easy. Teams that can walk that fine line, however, can bring out innovative insights from everyone on board.

Evernote, a cloud-based software company, owes its existence to such task-focused conflict. Evernote is an online note-taking program launched in 2008. Though the company's Redwood City, California, offices now bustle with laughter, things didn't exactly start that way. CEO Phil Libin says that the company was born out of conflict. Evernote began as two separate companies both looking to create a way for people to store information and recall it on demand, what is now referred to as a memory "extension." A serial entrepreneur, Libin had assembled his original team under the company name Ribbon but almost immediately learned of another team of mostly Russian programmers who called their project Evernote.[11] The Russian coders had already made significant progress on Libin's idea, so Libin proposed a merger. Rather than fight each other in the industry, the two companies joined forces and fought each other inside the same walls. "Evernote was created in this unusual way: two startups with similar visions but different personalities and backgrounds," Libin recalls.[12] "Immediately, we had a conflict of ideas, but that's what made it strong: Only the best ideas survive." The two teams kept their conflict focused on the overall mission of creating a product that simply and easily allows people to save notes and retrieve them from a variety of platforms like their phone, tablet, or computer. Even today, when conflict arises, it's usually in the service of Evernote's larger mission and not the smaller mission of individual interests.

In the 1970s at Xerox PARC, regularly scheduled arguments were routine.[13] The company that gave birth to the personal computer staged formal discussions designed to train their people on how to fight properly over ideas and not egos. PARC held weekly meetings they called "Dealer" (from a popular book of the time titled *Beat the Dealer*). Before each meeting, one person, known as "the dealer," was selected as the speaker. The speaker would present his idea and then try to defend it against a room of engineers and scientists determined to prove him wrong. Such debates helped improve products under development and sometimes resulted in wholly new ideas for future pursuit. The facilitators of the Dealer meetings were careful to make sure that only intellectual criticism of the merit of an idea received attention and consideration. Those in the audience or at the podium were never allowed to personally criticize their colleagues or bring their colleagues' character or personality into play. Bob Taylor, a former manager at PARC, said of their meetings, "If someone tried to push their personality rather than their argument, they'd find that it wouldn't work."[14] Inside these debates, Taylor taught his people the difference between what he called Class 1 disagreements, in which neither party understood the other party's true position, and Class 2 disagreements, in which each side could articulate the other's stance.[15] Class 1 disagreements were always discouraged, but Class 2 disagreements were allowed, as they often resulted in a higher quality of ideas. Taylor's model removed the personal friction from debates and taught individuals to use conflict as a means to find common, often higher, ground.

The teams at Pixar rely on their own method to keep their daily sessions focused on intellectual conflict and to avoid personal bickering. They call that method "plussing."[16] Whenever an idea is challenged or an animated frame criticized, that criticism must always contain a suggestion about how to improve the work—a plus. Suppose a team of animators and directors has assembled one morning to examine a few frames of footage in which one character smiles at another. If one animator challenges the type of smile the character gives, perhaps saying it looks inauthentic or as though the character is smiling but not legitimately happy, then she must also add suggestions for how that facial expression can be tweaked to be more authentic—perhaps tightening the sides of the character's eyes as the smile grows from frame to frame. Different animators and directors use different language when they plus their criticism. Some provide a specific suggestion; others might preface their suggestions with a "what if" such as, "What if his eyebrows arched as he smiled?" Regardless of the style

155

used, the result of plussing is always the same: it gives the criticized animator a new direction or something new to work with. The animators and directors on the receiving end of the plussing don't necessarily have to accept and incorporate the feedback, but plussing provides a method to share criticisms in a way that makes it more likely that they will. Just as the criticism groups in Nemeth's traffic study challenged each other and produced more ideas because of that, teams at Pixar challenge potential problems with a film and then plus their criticism, beginning the process of generating ideas for improvement. When animators leave the meetings, they can implement the ideas from plussing, or, as Nemeth's study suggests, they might come up with more ideas on the way back from the meeting and choose to implement those. In addition, plussing keeps the atmosphere inside the screening room positive and focuses the attention on the frame in question, not the animator who produced it.

Without plussing, their morning crit sessions could get pretty negative and emotionally draining. "You always want to present your ideas in a constructive manner and be respectful of the other animator's feelings," says Victor Navone, an animator at Pixar since 2000.[17] Animation is a labor-intensive process in and of itself, with long days spent producing less than a second of film. Knowing that the next morning your work will get torn apart and that then you'll be back at the drawing board (or computer) trying to repair the frames leaves little to look forward to. Ed Catmull explains, "And it's very important for that dynamic to work . . . [T]here needs to be the feeling they are all helping each other and the director wants that help."[18]

With plussing, the meetings are imbued with a positive tone and a direct connection between criticism and newer or better ideas for the work. Plussing doesn't ease all of the tension, however. It's always difficult to watch as your work is analyzed and criticized down to the smallest detail. But when that criticism is part of a larger end goal like an award-winning new film, it is a little easier to process. Pixar's dailies still feel like a fight, but they feel like the healthy, respectful fights that keep creative teams churning out quality work consistently.

It's easy to look at the output of a group like Pixar or Evernote and make assumptions about its creative process. The Cohesive Myth leads us to the assumption that if we want to be as creative as Pixar or make innovative products like Evernote, we need to build teams that are happy and playful all the time. Although the folks at both companies certainly enjoy their work and their teams, they also understand that conflict, not cohesion, can drive their creative process. When we focus too much on making our teams cohesive, we give up the creative boost that comes from having to defend an idea. We lose the ability to strengthen the idea through criticism. If instead we learn how to fight properly, how to use conflict to enhance our creative potential, then our teams and our organizations stand a better chance of generating consistently great ideas.

The Constraints Myth

When we think of the creative process, we tend to think of outlandish and unrestrained idea generation. We assume that the most creative organizations are full of unbounded workers with unlimited resources building the future however they see fit. We assume that creativity needs total freedom to grow and develop. These assumptions are made because of a belief in the *Constraints Myth*—the myth that creative potential is dampened by constraints. Many artists subscribe to this myth. They believe that if their creativity knew no bounds—if they had the time and resources to do as they pleased—then the work they created would be recognized for its genius. At the same time, we constantly affirm the need to "think outside the box," often without having fully explored the inside of it. The Constraints Myth actually provides a little comfort for when we're stuck on a creative challenge or complex problem. It provides a simple explanation for many of those frustrations: "It's not us;

it's our lack of resources." That explanation too often becomes an excuse, a crutch for those seeking to limp out of creative pursuits. The crutch is unsteady, however. There is no support for the idea that constraints hinder creativity. In fact, the research supports the opposite, and many innovative teams will tell you that creativity loves constraints.

Many of the most prolific and creative people understand how stifling a blank slate can be. All creatives need some constraints. All artists need structure. Some of the most creative poetry comes in fixed forms such as the Japanese haiku or the English sonnet. The fixed form becomes a framework that poets build from. The requirements set by these forms make the work more challenging, but that challenge pushes poets to meet their creative potential. Matthew May explains the phenomenon through sculpture: "Michelangelo's statue of David would not be considered the masterpiece it is had he chosen to mold it from clay rather than sculpt it from marble, a subtractive endeavor involving an unyielding and unforgiving material."[1] What Michelangelo was able to do through the constraining substance of marble is what draws crowds to see his work centuries later. Regardless of the field, constraints shape our creative pursuits. Ideas that are novel become useful because they can be easily applied inside the given constraints. Constraints provide us a structure through which to understand our problems and think of truly innovative solutions. That structure of constraints was just what a humanitarian and a group of college students needed to develop a unique type of peanut sheller.

In 2001, when Jock Brandis was doing humanitarian work with a friend in Mali, he learned that peanuts are hard nuts to crack. Brandis was building a water treatment system when he noticed many of the village women shelling peanuts by hand.[2] Peanuts were plentiful in the area and had become a source of food and income for the subsistence farmers Brandis was working to help. But shelling peanuts by hand is grueling work. It takes a long time to shell a decent load of peanuts. The splintering shells often made the women's fingers bleed, and the repetitive nature of the work left them likely to develop arthritis at an early age. After seeing how difficult the process was and the toll it took on the women in Mali, Brandis made a promise to one of the women in the village where he was working. He promised her that he would get her a peanut sheller when he returned to the United States. However, when he did return, Brandis ran into a bit of a problem. What he was looking for didn't exist. Brandis couldn't locate any small-scale peanut shellers, only the large-scale machinery equipment used by commercial peanut farmers. There wasn't a market for small shellers in the developed world, and the developing world couldn't afford the large ones that did exist.

Undeterred by the lack of small peanut shellers, Brandis set to work building his own. However, he was up against a serious constraint: cost. It would do no good to design a small-scale peanut sheller at a price that subsistence farmers couldn't afford. He contacted peanut experts and engineers and eventually discovered a Bulgarian design for a small-scale peanut sheller. Brandis had to modify the design to remove costly components but still keep its essential function. After several iterations, he had completed what he called the Malian Peanut Sheller (now called the Universal Nut Sheller). Brandis's device is relatively simple, but its potential impact on subsistence farmers in the developing world is huge. The device speeds up the process of shelling peanuts dramatically and does so without inflicting trauma to the farmers' hands. And Brandis's unique design lowered the cost dramatically. Instead of costing hundreds of dollars, it can be made for less than $50 from materials that are typically readily available or easy to import. The machine is already being used by people in seventeen different countries to increase their incomes and improve their lives.

But the Universal Nut Sheller isn't perfect. Once it's made, the device is sturdy and efficient, but making one is not the most efficient process. The main component of the machine is made from concrete that is poured into fiberglass molds to harden. Although in most countries it's not difficult to get the various materials needed to manufacture the machine, these fiberglass molds are hard to make in developing nations. Instead, they are usually shipped from the United States, and this shipment increases the price of the machine as well as the time it takes to build one. That's where Lonny Grafman entered the picture to solve the next problem.

Grafman is an engineering professor at Humboldt State University who partnered with Brandis in an attempt to improve upon several projects, including the nut sheller. Grafman was particularly drawn to the country of Haiti, which had problems with plastic waste polluting its ecosystem. In the landfills and along the beaches of Haiti were vast quantities of plastic trash bags.[3] Grafman challenged his students to turn this plastic waste into a replacement for the fiberglass molds that concrete would be poured into to make the nut shellers. After a few weeks of hard work, Grafman's students came to him defeated. They told Grafman that his challenge could not be met. The plastic could be melted down to make a mold, but doing so would release toxic gases into the air. The students had hit an enormous constraint. They had to develop a method for melting or shaping the plastic within a temperature range that wouldn't emit the toxic gas. But Grafman wouldn't admit defeat. He told the students that there was always a solution to be found, so there was a way to make the process work.

The very next day, his students found a solution that worked within the temperature constraint. Instead of melting the bags down to make the mold, they found they could slice the bags into thin plastic rings and weave these together to make a plastic fabric. This fabric could be heated using a simple iron and shaped into the right form. Because the bags wouldn't be melted entirely, the gases would not be released. Grafman's students not only solved the toxic gases problem but also found a way to reduce the cost of Brandis's nut sheller even further by using readily available waste material. Haitians could now build the entire nut sheller using materials available on the island while simultaneously reducing the presence of plastic waste in their landfills and on their beaches.

Brandis's original design and Grafman's students' improvements are both vivid illustrations of what creative, motivated people can accomplish. However, they also illustrate something more. The stories are so compelling because they involve several individuals working with what many believe is the chief hindrance to creativity: constraints. It would have been easy for Brandis and Grafman's students to admit defeat when faced with these constraints. But in reality, constraints often force us to be more creative, not less so. The constraints actually helped them build a better end product. By insisting that the nut sheller's mold be created from plastic waste, Grafman applied a constraint that forced his team of students to consider alternatives that would not have been obvious otherwise, and the students had to get more creative in order to find a solution. Innovation doesn't stem from wide-open spaces or from thinking outside the box. Instead, innovation happens when people work from inside the box, sometimes rethinking and reshaping the box entirely.

The Constraints Myth is easy to accept and readily believed. It even seems rational given what we know about intrinsic motivation and its effect on creativity. No one enjoys spending a lot of time on projects that seem hopeless. However, research on the creative process across multiple domains supports the opposing perspective on constraints. "Many people freeze if they are given a blank piece of paper," notes Teresa Amabile, who has seen that freezing many times during her research career.[4] "But if they are given a blank sheet of paper with a squiggly line on it and asked to elaborate on that squiggle, they often have fun turning out something pretty interesting." The squiggly line challenge is actually a hallmark of many creativity assessments. Amabile's point is that some constraints often aid the creative process and increase the quality of work produced.

Constraints provide a starting point and a problem to solve. Both are necessary for producing creative insights. Many times the presence of constraints aids our ability to generate novel ideas and shapes their usefulness to the world around us. This is a hard truth for some to accept: that a lack of resources may not be their true constraint, just a lack of resourcefulness.

As in the story of the trash bag peanut sheller, sometimes constraints themselves can be a resource for solving problems. Psychologist Patricia Stokes believes that constraints actually help by providing us with a structure to understand the problem and evaluate solutions. Stokes has taken a rather creative route to becoming a psychology professor. After earning a bachelor's degree in social science, Stokes pivoted and began a new career as an art student at Pratt Institute. After graduation, she went to work for advertising giant J. Walter Thompson and found herself working on campaigns for national brands such as Avon, Maybelline, and even Wonder Bread. Stokes traveled the world and lived abroad for several years. She was living the dream of a successful creative when something inside her changed. "It was terrific for a long time," Stokes says. "And then something terrible happened—I got bored."[5]

To combat her boredom, Stokes went back to school. But instead of studying more art or diverting to pair an MBA in marketing with her MFA in painting, Stokes chose psychology. She earned a PhD from Columbia University. She now teaches psychology at Barnard College in Columbia University and runs the Variability and Creativity Lab there. Stokes has become an influential researcher in creativity precisely because of her unusual path to psychology. Now she finds herself studying the psychology behind what she had been doing for years as a creative professional. Because of her background, Stokes was particularly interested in studying how the constraints of a specific medium like paint or television affect the creative process. After years of research, Stokes has concluded that constraints exert a huge influence on our creative ability and that that influence is actually quite positive. Stokes has studied the creative process in a diverse set of fields, including art, literature, music, and advertising, and found that because they work within certain constraints, creative people don't do things *that* differently from the established norms. They work inside or at the edges of the metaphorical box, but rarely outside it. Stokes argues that creativity actually requires some constraints and that the presence of constraints has made possible many of the most innovative works of our time, whether they be in art or advertising.[6]

All of us, it turns out, think inside self-imposed constraints. Here's a quick thought experiment to demonstrate: picture the future. Better yet, picture the future as portrayed in movies from the 1960s. In that future, the cars look largely the same, except maybe they fly. The television seems the same, except the people on the screen are dressed oddly. The homes look almost identical except sparkly clean. Ever wonder why the future imagined in the 1960s looked so much like a shiner version of the 1960s? Even if you imagined your own future, there's a good chance that it more closely resembles the present than what you'll actually find. That's because all of us have a self-imposed notion that the future will evolve neatly from the present.[7] We actually constrain ourselves to think linearly and don't consider what disruptive innovations will occur. The envisioned future is just one example of a fundamental tendency of human cognition: we imagine from within the comfortable constraints of our own experience. If we're given free rein to be creative or to solve a problem, we typically end up focusing on what we know or what's worked in the past. Even if we had the unlimited resources or the unhindered creativity we claim to want, we'd end up imposing other constraints anyway. Constraints are a part of our life, and they are a comforting part. Stokes's thesis is that because most of us face constraints anyway, learning how to strategically use those constraints promotes a more creative outcome than roaming entirely free.[8]

Granted, not all constraints have the same effect on creativity. Some do in fact hinder creative expression. If the box is too small, then thinking inside it won't fit very many possibilities. But other constraints can end up yielding creative breakthroughs. Stokes's research has revealed four constraints that promote creativity: domain constraints, cognitive constraints, variability constraints, and talent constraints.

Domain constraints are those imposed by oneself or the field one operates in. Regardless of the field, everyone requires a certain level of understanding before he or she can contribute novel and original ideas. In many fields, there are agreed-on performance standards or standard operating procedures for any work produced. Painting requires paint. Music requires notes and scales. These examples are overly simplistic, but they demonstrate the nature of domain constraints. Domain constraints promote creativity by providing a structure that people can work within and a standard against which they can produce variations. This is why many creative individuals sometimes set their own domain constraints. They limit variability and make it easier for others in the domain to appreciate the new work. Stokes refers to these constraints as the "first chorus," after how the first chorus in a musical piece usually sets the melody for the rest of the piece.[9] Even if you deviate from the first chorus, that deviation draws its significance from what it is not.

Cognitive constraints come from the limitations of the mind, both the creator's and that of the audience. Oftentimes a creative work is misunderstood or overlooked simply because people cannot process it against their past experiences. Creative ideas have to be novel and useful, and that usefulness is judged against the cognitive constraints of the beholder. Consider the infamous Pets.com Super Bowl commercial of 2000. The ad championed the slogan "Because Pets Can't Drive" as an answer to why people should buy pet supplies online. The ad was certainly novel and very comical. It even became the highest-ranked commercial of that Super Bowl on *USA Today's* "Ad Meter." Yet it failed the ultimate test of utility in advertising: sales. Few people who saw the ad were convinced they needed to buy dog food online. The ad's creators believed their pitch would be enough, but their belief stemmed from a lack of understanding about their audience, which didn't weigh the driving ability of pets as a reason for them to try shopping for pet food online. Becoming an expert in a given domain helps creators overcome cognitive limitations and understand which ideas are most likely to also be useful. However, being an expert doesn't excuse them from ignoring the cognitive constraints of their audience.

Variability constraints consider how much a given piece of work or creative process needs to vary from the existing standards. Exact copies aren't recognized as creative, though copies with unique modifications can be. Variability constraints help creators understand just how different their work needs to be to meet the "novel" requirement for creativity. They reveal the fine line between copying and creating. Legendary heavy metal band Led Zeppelin is still engulfed in controversy about which of its songs are uniquely original and which are uncredited cover songs. For example, the opening of their most famous song, "Stairway to Heaven," sounds remarkably similar to a song by the group Spirit, "Taurus," which was written three years prior.[10] It doesn't help Led Zeppelin's argument for originality that they even toured with Spirit in the years before releasing "Stairway to Heaven." Variability constraints differ greatly across industries and creative genres, just as the tolerance for mimicry differs across fields.

Talent constraints refer to the abilities that Stokes believes are genetic. Although creativity in general is not a genetically given talent, other abilities that aid creative people in their work likely are genetic traits. Tone-deaf individuals will have a significant disadvantage in musical composition, whereas it is much easier for those born with near perfect pitch. Likewise, colorblind artists will have a harder time capturing the variety of shades needed in a quality still life. Stokes is quick to note, though, that talent does not guarantee creativity and that it is hardly the sole predictor of creative ability. We're still sorting out which talents are natural and which can be developed. However, Stokes argues that even those abilities that can be developed are often acquired at different rates for different individuals due to talent constraints.

Stokes believes that these four constraints aid creativity by providing a structure that helps solve creative problems. In many fields, there are ill-structured problems that are left unresolved or problems with little hope of a resolution, such as a "unified theory of everything" in physics.[11] While physicists are actively looking for a single theory to explain everything in the universe, every new discovery adds a level of complexity to the rubric against which a theory of everything would be measured. We don't yet know everything about the universe, so we don't know our constraints. It is thus difficult to develop a theory to explain everything. Ill-structured problems are difficult precisely because they don't have constraints. Just as when we try to envision the future, ill-structured problems reduce our solutions to what has worked in the past. When constraints are applied that limit our ability to return to these past solutions, they force us think more creatively.

The creativity-boosting power of constraints doesn't just come from the fact that they provide a structure to work within. In turns out that when our minds encounter constraints, we're better able to tap into our creative potential. Psychology researchers at the University of Amsterdam recently showed that people open their minds to more creative ideas and better connect unrelated thoughts after they encoun-

170

ter constraints.[12] The researchers divided participants into two groups. The participants in both groups began first by playing a computer game that challenged them to escape from a maze on the screen. One of the groups, however, played a modified version of the maze that severely limited participants' options and made escape a much harder endeavor. Their game was significantly constrained by the lack of options. After the maze game, both groups of participants were given a standard creativity assessment consisting of several puzzles designed to test their ability to draw connections among seemingly unrelated thoughts. The participants who tried to escape the more difficult maze ended up solving 40 percent more puzzles than the group that played with a simpler maze. The researchers concluded that the constraints in the harder maze also triggered a response in the participants' minds, which heightened their imaginative abilities. What these researchers have discovered about the creativity-enhancing power of facing constraints, some companies have already known and implemented. These organizations willingly embrace constraints. One such company, 37signals, goes beyond tolerating constraints for the sake of greater creativity. It creates them.

Chances are good that before it was mentioned in Chapter Six, you had never heard of software company 37signals. But the company has generated lots of publicity within technology circles for its contrarian views, its criticism of most tech startups, and its willingness to work within self-imposed constraints. With Jason Fried at the helm, 37signals was founded in 1999 as a website design firm that specialized in creating websites for businesses.[13] From nearly the beginning, the group utilized an alternative billing approach that forced them to work within constraints. Many website developers at the time billed by the hour or bid on large-scale, long-term products with high price tags. Instead, Fried's group billed $3,500 per Web page built, and offered to complete the page inside of one week.[14] If the client wanted to add another page, the price was another $3,500 and another week. Adopting this format forced Fried's team to work efficiently inside the constraints of time and medium—they had only one page, one week, and $3,500 in labor costs with which to develop their product. The offering took off. In addition to developing creative Web pages, 37signals' constrained pricing allowed companies to minimize the risk they took on a Web developer. Businesses liked that they could bet a small amount on 37signals and that if it didn't work out, they could look elsewhere. Most of the time, though, it worked out better than expected.

In 2003, the 37signals business model began to change dramatically. It was then that Fried first hired David Heinemeier Hansson as a contractor to develop a project management system for 37signals to use internally.[15] The program worked so well for the company's purposes that it decided to release it as a commercial product. In 2004, Basecamp, the company's flagship project management tool, was launched. By 2012, Basecamp was being used by millions of people to manage over eight million projects,[16] from Fortune 500 companies' product launches to presidential campaigns.[17] "When we were building Basecamp," Fried and Hansson write, "we had plenty of limitations. We had a design firm to run with existing client work, a seven-hour time difference between principals (David was doing the programming in Denmark, the rest of us were in the States), a small team, and no outside funding."[18] Fried and Hansson believed that these constraints didn't really limit their capability. Instead, they helped them create a beautiful product because "these constraints forced us to keep the product simple."

Although it was initially just a response to the constraint of resources, the simplicity of their Basecamp product became a self-imposed domain constraint for 37signals. Basecamp was such a usable product because it was so simple. The developers didn't have the resources to build a feature-laden product, so they didn't. What they found was that users didn't want all those features; they wanted something that was simple to work with. Any new iteration of Basecamp, or any 37signals product, has to stay simple to use. The company currently offers only four core products: Highrise (a customer relationship management tool), Campfire (a real-time group chat room for business collaboration), Backpack (an information manager and intranet), and Basecamp. Each of these products is simple, effective, and devoid of the "feature creep" of most software tools. The initial lack of resources has turned into the keystone of the company's success. "These days, we have more resources and people, but we still force constraints," Fried and Hansson write. "We make sure to have only one or two people working on a product at a time. And we always keep features to a minimum. Boxing ourselves in this way prevents us from creating bloated products."[19]

In addition to its self-imposed constraint of simplicity, 37signals has also found freedom inside another self-imposed constraint: pricing. Although its product pricing is tiered depending on usage, the company places a maximum possible price on what any single customer will pay for a given product. For Basecamp, that price is $150 per month. Regardless of the number of user accounts a customer creates or how much the product is used, the price will never exceed $150. This pricing constraint isn't a marketing ploy, either. Fried has found that this arrangement puts his mind more at ease and allows the entire company to focus on providing great service and making great products. "Lots of business owners spend their lives trying to land the whale—the single, massive, brand name account that will fatten the top line and bestow instant credibility. But big customers make me nervous,"[20] Fried writes. "After all, he who pays you the most has the most control over you. And we don't want any one customer to control us." While this constraint may force them to stay extra lean, it also frees them to focus their creativity on developing great products, not entertaining large clients.

37signals' enthusiastic embrace of constraints seems to be working. Its simple, elegant products generate several million dollars in revenue a year.[21] Its success is remarkable in light of another self-imposed constraint: 37signals hasn't accepted a single dollar of venture capital funding in its lifetime. Fried and Hansson believe that most outside capital is a polluting influence, and, although the resources would be nice, the pressure to turn a profit, sell the company, or make an initial public offering would be distracting.

There is a lot 37signals can't do. It's not likely to become a giant tech company like Microsoft, Apple, or Google. The constraints produced by its lean emphasis won't allow it to throw hordes of cash at solving problems or improving products. However, it willingly embraces these difficulties because it is these difficulties that have produced much of the success 37signals has experienced in the company's ten-plus-year existence. The lack of resources has served as the trigger for the creative and elegant solutions the company has developed while creating or improving products. "Constraints are advantages in disguise," Fried and Hansson write. "Limited resources force you to make do with what you've got. There's no room for waste. And that forces you to be creative."[22]

There's a good chance that Fried and Hansson have never heard of Patricia Stokes's research on constraints and creativity. However, there's an equally good chance that Stokes's advice to those who complain about lack of resources would be the same as 37signals': "Stop whining. Less is a good thing."[23] Despite their admonition, many of us prefer to whine. We see our setbacks and creative difficulties and revel in the Constraints Myth. We want an outside explanation for why we aren't more creative, and constraints are an easy excuse to cite. In organizations, this belief leads to stalled-out projects and little innovation. It leads to teams focused on finding more resources and eliminating constraints instead of working inside those constraints and boosting their creativity. If we believe the Constraints Myth and focus on solving the problem of getting more resources, then we divert our attention away from the original problem. Instead, the evidence suggests that we should lean into constraints and focus on the structure they provide around our problem. From Lonny Grafman's college engineering class to world-class companies like 37signals, the most innovative people and companies embrace constraints and focus their creative attention on coming up with solutions that work inside set limitations. Creativity doesn't just love constraints; it thrives under them.

11

The Mousetrap Myth

If you build a better mousetrap, the world will beat a path to your door. We've all heard that saying before. It's become quite a popular maxim. It's a catchy line, and it offers some hope to those who are working on seemingly great ideas. But it also turns out to be really bad advice. In fact, that saying is the perfect encapsulation of the *Mousetrap Myth*. Belief in this myth is built on the assumption that once you have a creative idea or innovative new product, getting others to see its value is the easy part, and that if you develop a great idea, the world will willingly embrace it. We expect a celebration when the product launches or our new work is on display. But this is often not the case. In fact, it is rarely the case. A belief in the Mousetrap Myth sets us up for disappointment, because the world's most common reaction to a new idea isn't to beat a path to our door. It's typically to beat down the idea or, perhaps worse, ignore it.

Consider the actual mousetrap. The U.S. Patent Office has issued over forty-four hundred patents for better versions of the mousetrap;[1] of those, only about twenty designs have ever been developed into a commercially viable product. The most successful design, by far, is the spring trap we all envision in our heads. This version was designed in 1899. Despite the roughly four hundred additional mousetrap designs submitted for a new patent every year, no design has yet surpassed the spring trap. Behind all these issued designs is a simple truth: even if you can build a better mousetrap, there is still a lot of work involved in selling the world on your new design. That is the lesson Admiral William Sowden Sims of the U.S. Navy learned when he discovered a new method that would revolutionize naval battles but found that the hardest battle was convincing his superiors of the validity of that new method.

Sims's innovation came from a single great idea that, when implemented, would drastically improve the accuracy and efficiency of gunfire at sea—except that it wasn't implemented, at least at first.[2] To understand the nature of Sims's innovation, you first have to understand the difficulties of firing a weapon at sea. The main problem is that every gun is mounted on the deck of a rolling ship, a platform that is, by its nature, unstable. Before 1898, every gun on every ship used the same technique to attempt to work with this instability. The gun pointer would take aim at a target through his sights and then adjust the elevation of the gun to meet the range of his desired target. As he aimed the gun, he would watch the target as the roll of the ship moved it up and down in his sights. When the target moved back into his crosshairs, he would fire. This method was not without some significant flaws, however. The first was that the gun pointer had to allow the movement of the ship to dictate the speed of his firing. Because he relied on the rolls of the ship to bring the target into his sights, he could fire only as often as the waves rolled the target ship into his crosshairs. In addition, even though he was trained to fire when the target came into his sights, there was enough of a delay between his intent to fire and his actually pressing the firing button that by the time the button was pushed, the roll of the ocean was likely to skew his aim.

Sims's innovation was actually the idea of an English naval officer, Admiral Sir Percy Scott, who had developed it during his tenure as captain of the HMS *Scylla* from 1896 to 1899. One day, Scott was observing target practice in the midst of particularly rough seas. Given the conditions, most of the gun pointers were performing terribly, with the exception of one man. Scott saw how the man kept his hands on the elevating gear constantly. Even when peering through his sights, the man used his hand to make subtle adjustments to his elevation by manipulating the gears. Because of these subtle manipulations, the man's target stayed within his crosshairs even as the ship rolled up and down. Scott resolved to find a way for every gun pointer on his ship to learn to fire like that man. He set about redesigning all the *Scylla*'s guns to make it easier for those pointing them to continuously make small adjustments to the gun's angle while the ship was rolling. These changes allowed the pointers to keep a target in their sights despite the pace and intensity of the rolling waves. Scott's technological changes and new firing method became known as continuous-aim firing.

Two years later, while stationed in China on the HMS *Terrible*, Scott met William S. Sims, at the time a junior officer in the U.S. Navy. The two men bonded quickly, and Scott told Sims about his experiments and successes with continuous-aim firing. With Scott's help, Sims modified the gear on his own ship and retrained his crew to use the new system. Within a few months, Sims's crew had begun setting exceptional accuracy records in target practice. Sims knew he had stumbled on an outstanding method and tried immediately to share that method with the entire American fleet. But the fleet's senior leaders showed little of the excitement Sims had for the innovation. In fact, they showed none.

Over time, Sims compiled and sent thirteen official reports to both the Bureau of Ordinance and the Bureau of Navigation outlining the method he'd adopted and documenting the success rate of Scott's ships and his own. At first, the bureaus in Washington didn't respond. They had read the reports, but concluded that Sims's statements were fabricated. They dismissed the reports, filed them away, and did not even take the time to respond to Sims's claim. With each report, Sims's language grew harsher and his tactics more deviant. He began sending copies of his report to other officers in the fleet to spread the word in the hopes that the higher-ups in Washington would have to respond. Eventually, they did respond. The chief of the Bureau of Ordinance responded by flatly denying Sims's claims. He argued that the standard American equipment was as good as the British fleet's and that the target practice records set using Sims's method of continuous-aim firing were mathematically impossible. The problem with this denial was that Sims had already proven his method through numerous trials, and other officers were reproducing his results on their own ships.

Eventually, Sims wrote a final report and sent it to President Theodore Roosevelt along with a letter explaining himself, his idea, and the trials he had faced getting his idea implemented across the Navy. Roosevelt in the past had served a brief period as assistant secretary of the Navy. Perhaps it was that history that caused him to take action when he read the letter and learned how Sims's constant attempts to improve Navy gunnery were being ignored. But whatever the reason, Roosevelt saw the merit in Sims's claim and immediately ordered him to Washington. Roosevelt had Sims installed as the inspector of target practice for the entire Navy. Sims was finally in a position to implement his method. At the end of his six years as inspector, he was universally known throughout the Navy as "the man who taught us how to shoot."

Creative ideas, by their very nature, invite judgment. People need to know if the value promised by the new is worth the abandonment of the old. We tend to fear change, and therefore we fear the innovations that call us to change. In organizations especially, we're told to have fresh ideas and to think outside the box. However, in the rare cases when individuals actually do propose something unique, their idea is often rejected as being too outlandish or impossible.

The other problem is that people worry that if they share their creative ideas, then those ideas will be stolen and someone else will take the credit for their innovation. Howard H. Aiken, a renowned innovator and pioneer in computing, held the opposite view. Aiken's advice for those favoring creative secrecy was, "Don't worry about people stealing yours ideas. If your ideas are any good, you'll have to ram them down people's throats."[3] His own experience shaped his belief that people inherently reject, not adopt or steal, creative ideas. Aiken isn't alone in this experience or in giving this advice. Eric Ries, a serial entrepreneur and adviser to numerous start-ups, says he often encounters would-be entrepreneurs worried to truly begin their endeavor for fear that potential competitors will steal their ideas and destroy their market share. Ries says, "I have often given entrepreneurs fearful of this issue the following assignment: take one of your ideas (one of your lesser insights, perhaps), find the name of the relevant product manager at an established company who has responsibility for that area, and try to get that company to steal your idea."[4] Ries explains the rationale behind his assignment this way: "The truth is that most managers in most companies are already overwhelmed with good ideas." While we may fear that our great ideas will be stolen, it's most likely that they will be ignored. In the cases where an idea is considered, it's still more likely that it will be rejected than stolen.

The examples of great ideas being utterly rejected are plentiful. Kodak's research laboratory invented the first digital camera in 1975 but didn't pursue it. Kodak didn't believe that people would be willing to give up the quality produced by film pictures.[5] The original prototype weighed several pounds and had a resolution of 0.01 megapixels. It was built from the

lens of another camera, a tape recorder, and a random assortment of found parts. When it was presented to the managers
at Kodak, it was immediately sent back to the lab and eventually shelved. Management had decided that the immediate
future was still in film because film offered a superior resolution. Kodak paid no attention as Sony developed a different
prototype and stole the future of digital photography out from
underneath it. When Sony presented its first digital camera,
which was hailed as a history-making technological innovation
even though it lacked the resolution of film, Kodak still showed
no signs of interest. "Why would anyone want a still camera
that takes pictures only as sharp as those on your TV?" Kodak
vice president John Robertson said in response when Sony
unveiled its camera. "It's an idea we've discussed for years and
clearly decided that there's no market for the product."

In 2001, physician John Adler's nearly twenty-year struggle
against rejection ended when the FDA granted approval for
his breakthrough method for treating cancer that had to overcome nearly two decades of resistance.[6] Adler was studying in
Sweden when he noticed that surgeons there were using small
beams of radiation directed from multiple angles to attack
brain tumors. The radiation of each beam was weak enough
not to damage healthy tissue, but when the beams crossed at
the site of the tumor, the radiation accumulated and killed
the cancerous tissue. Adler developed a similar method for
treating cancer throughout the entire body using computers
to calculate the precise angles and strengths of multiple radiation beams. Adler's idea was ingenious, but his experience in
developing and selling the idea was lacking, and he struggled

to find anyone willing to fund the development or to purchase the end product. Those who gave Adler time to pitch his idea rejected it. It took Adler nearly two decades to find enough support to develop a viable prototype and business model for his idea. Today, however, what was once known as "Adler's Folly" is now known as "Cyberknife" and is used in almost every major cancer treatment center as an effective means for destroying tumors that would otherwise require invasive surgery.

Nobel laureate Paul C. Lauterbur found the Mousetrap Myth especially prevalent in the sciences. After a paper of his concerning the development of the MRI (for which he was later awarded the Nobel Prize) was initially rejected by the journal *Nature*, Lauterbur responded by saying, "You can write an entire history of science in the last 50 years in terms of papers rejected by *Science* or *Nature*."[7] Lauterbur's sentiment suggests that even experts in a given field have a tendency to reject the ideas that move the field forward. Ken Olsen, founder of Digital Equipment Corporation, once said, "There is no reason anyone would want a computer in their home."[8] Charles Duell, former head of the U.S. Patent Office, claimed in 1899 that "everything that can be invented has been invented."[9] Ironically, that was the same year that the patent for the spring-loaded mousetrap was issued. H. M. Warner, founder of movie giant Warner Brothers, disregarded the idea of talking pictures, saying, "Who the hell wants to hear actors talk?"[10] Even Socrates and Plato debated the idea that books would be a useful tool for transferring knowledge.[11] These are entertaining anecdotes, but they illustrate much more than the fact that intelligent people can be hilariously wrong when judging new ideas. They suggest that perhaps even the smartest among us have a hard time recognizing truly creative ideas.

Creative ideas make people uncomfortable. It turns out that, at least subconsciously, we can have a hard time recognizing ideas as both new and useful at the same time. This cognitive dissonance between creativity and practicality may actually create a subtle bias against creative ideas. This bias was empirically proven in 2012 by a single team of researchers from Cornell, Penn, and the University of North Carolina.[12] The research team, led by Jennifer Mueller, assistant professor of management at Penn's Wharton School of Finance, conducted two studies that examined our perceptions of creative ideas when we're faced with even the smallest amount of uncertainty. In the first study, the team divided participants into two groups and created a small level of uncertainty in one group by telling them they would be eligible for additional payment based on a random lottery of participants. The researchers didn't give many specifics around how their chance for additional payment would work, just that they would find out once the study was completed. It was hardly an earth-shattering proposition, but it was still enough to yield some feelings of uncertainty within the group. The participants were then given a series of tests. In the first test, participants were presented with word pairings on a computer and asked to select their preferred pairing. The pairings always included one word that was either creative or practical (words such as "novel," "original," "functional," or "useful") and one word that was either good or bad (words such as "sunshine," "peace," "ugly," or "war"). So in each round, participants would choose their preference between pairs like "useful war" or "novel sunshine." The test, known as an implicit associations test, uses the speed of participants' reaction time to measure the strength of their mental associations. The more quickly and more often participants tended toward certain combinations of words (such as good practical phrases or good creative ones), the higher their level of positive association with the concept. The second test was more overt; it measured participants' perceptions about creativity by asking them to rate their attitudes toward creativity and practicality on a seven-point scale. It's a straightforward method known as an explicit associations test. Both groups were given the same tests, but when the researchers calculated the results, they found that the group given no chance at extra compensation held both implicitly and explicitly positive associations between creativity and practicality. They said they desired creative ideas in the explicit tests, and, in the implicit tests, they didn't significantly favor creative phrases over practical ones. The uncertainty group, however, was a little different. This group held an explicitly positive association between the two, but implicitly their mind separated creative from practical. They had an implicit bias against creativity relative to practicality. While they said they valued creative ideas, when faced with a choice between a creative or a practical phrase on the implicit test, they tended to favor the practical. Participants in this group claimed to desire new, creative ideas, but when exposed to even the slightest bit of uncertainty, they significantly favored phrases that seemed less creative and more practical.

If this bias is present in everyone during periods of uncertainty, then it might explain why society has a history of rejecting notable innovations. To test this thesis, the research team returned to the lab and this time studied the ability of a new group of participants to judge a creative product idea. The participants were again divided into two groups. This time, the researchers would attempt to develop a high tolerance for uncertainty in one group and low tolerance in the other. Both groups were asked to prepare something in advance of the test in order to create this high or low tolerance for uncertainty. The high-tolerance group was asked to write an essay supporting the idea that multiple solutions existed for every problem. The intent of this was to "prime" the group by creating favoritism toward new ideas in the minds of the participants. To prime the low-tolerance group, the researchers asked those individuals to write an essay arguing the opposite—that most problems had only one right solution. The two groups were given the same implicit and explicit association tests as the first study and then asked to rate a creative idea for a new product, a running shoe that automatically adjusted its fabric thickness to keep the foot cool in changing temperature conditions. As anticipated by the first study, the low-tolerance group showed the same implicit bias against creativity and was also more likely to rate the running shoe idea poorly.

These results have some interesting implications for our views on creativity. Regardless of how open-minded people are or claim to be, they experience a subtle bias against creativity in uncertain situations. This isn't merely a preference for the familiar or a desire to maintain the status quo. It's an outright rejection of new, innovative ideas. Even when we want positive change, this bias affects our ability to recognize the creative ideas we claim to desire. Within organizations, recognizing creativity becomes even more complicated, as most ideas travel through an approval process involving multiple people in multiple levels of the organization. At each level, managers or teams have to decide whether the idea is viable and, perhaps more important to them, whether the idea has the potential to harm their own business units or careers. If it does, then it's just too risky to pursue. This effect is what David Owens, Vanderbilt professor for the practice of management and innovation, calls the "hierarchy of no."[13] These organizations extol the benefits of creativity and innovation, but those benefits are rejected because of the biases present in the same people who make up these organizations. Many organizations that consider themselves innovative might allow ideas time to develop, but they eventually force those ideas through hurdles intended to identify the best ideas for implementation. The problems occur when those hurdles are too high and when the bias against creativity filters out the ideas that would prove useful but are too novel to win approval. Mueller and her team even suggest that perhaps these organizations don't need more creative ideas; they may just need to develop a better system for identifying innovations and accepting creativity.[14] One company, founded by two friends and fellow refugees from traditional bureaucracy, has developed such a system.

Rite-Solutions is a software company based in Newport, Rhode Island.[15] The company makes a diverse range of software programs, from submarine command systems for the Navy to electronic gambling systems for casinos. It was started in 2000 by longtime friends Jim Lavoie and Joe Marino. The two had worked together at a leading defense contractor, and both had gone quite far within the company. But during their tenure, they'd grown increasingly frustrated with the way their company handled innovative ideas. "If you had a great idea, we would tell you, 'Okay, we'll make an appointment for you to address the murder board,'" Lavoie says. "The murder board's job was to make sure the company took no risk. Their job was to shoot down ideas."[16] These murder boards, Marino recalls, would assault the idea person with questions about market size, cost projections, or estimated return on investment. Against such an assault, it wasn't necessarily the best ideas or the best people who got a green light; it was the best presenters. "I made it to executive VP not by being bright, but by being theatrical," Lavoie says.[17]

Lavoie and Marino wanted to establish a different kind of company, one where new ideas would be welcomed and cultivated, instead of shut down upon their initial hearing. Although the company was founded with this goal in mind, it wasn't until 2004 that they knew how to develop such a system.[18] Lavoie was listening to the financial news and thinking about the stock market when he began to wonder if markets could be a tool for judging innovation. In a market, anyone can invest in whatever company he or she feels has promise. Individuals study their potential investments and, when they feel they know enough, chose to get involved by buying stock. There is no murder board that hears the business plans of each stock and decides how many people are allowed to invest. Lavoie thought that he could build a similar system inside their company for managing the innovative ideas of his people. The "Mutual Fun" was born.

The Mutual Fun was a market-like system set up on Rite-Solutions' internal website. They divided this market into three exchanges for classifying ideas. The "Spazdaq" features ideas with considerable risk, usually entirely new businesses or technologies. The "Bow Jones" is for potential extensions on existing products, and the "Savings Bonds" is for small-scale operational innovations. Anyone in the company can place his or her idea on any of these three markets. No one needs to get approval from management before listing an idea. For every idea listed, the idea's champion creates an "ExpectUs" (a pun on "prospectus") that describes the idea and its potential. Each stock also has a "Budge-It" that outlines the steps the idea's champion believes must be taken to move (budge) the idea forward. The new stock is given a starting price of $10 and even assigned a ticker symbol. Each employee is also given $10,000 in virtual currency to invest in whatever ideas intrigue him or her. In addition to receiving investment money, each stock listing also has a comments thread so that the merits of the idea and any next steps that need to be considered can be discussed.

Just like in a real market, investment money flows unevenly to the ideas that investors favor and that they feel have the best chance of becoming viable projects. But employees don't just invest money; they also volunteer their time and expertise to help potential projects. Once a week, a "market maker" logs into the system and revalues each stock based on the money invested and the time committed. Ideas that fail to attract enough interest are eventually removed. Ideas that gain momentum are given actual funding to help them develop into real projects. When a stock moves from an idea to a moneymaking project, those who have invested their time get to share in the proceeds through bonuses or stock options in the actual company. Anyone who lists an idea, even if it generates no investment, is given credit for doing so on his or her annual performance evaluation.

Even though it's been only a few years since its launch in 2005, the system has already become a huge success. The $10,000 given to each employee might be virtual currency, but the return on investment pays in real dollars. "It lets us harvest the collective brilliance of everyone," Lavoie says. In one instance, the company's core technology of pattern-recognizing algorithms was given a huge boost when it was applied to a new market because of an idea that started on the Mutual Fun. The algorithms were being used for various military applications and casino gaming programs. Then a member of the administrative staff, someone with no technical knowledge about how these algorithms worked, wondered if they could be used to create educational games as well.[19] She listed the idea on the Mutual Fun, where it received a rush of investments from engineers eager to see it work. The idea was developed, and it led to a major contract with a leading toy company. In its first year alone, the Mutual Fun accounted for 50 percent of the company's new business growth.[20]

What Rite-Solutions has created is a way to manage the ideas of its people while undermining the bias against creativity found in most organizations. Instead of having to run through an assembled murder board or a hierarchy of no, each idea is presented before the entire company within a system designed to allow the best ideas to float upward. The decision to pursue an idea isn't left to a few people holding all the power and hence taking all the risk of uncertainty. Instead of forcing a yes-or-no answer from someone in management, this approach spreads the weight of these large decisions throughout the company. If you're intrigued by the idea but not enthralled by it, you invest some money but not your time. According to Marino, the program has another benefit for him as chief decision maker: "This system removes the terrible burden of always having to be right."[21] The weight of uncertainty produced when evaluating an idea's potential is reduced. What Rite-Solutions hasn't done is to try overtly to *make* its people more creative. Lavoie and Marino believe that potential already exists inside each of their employees. They believe that instead of trying to enhance the creative output of the organization, they just had to get out of their own way and develop a better system for recognizing creative ideas.

It's not enough to merely generate great ideas. Though we live in a world of complex challenges and our organizations need innovative solutions, we also live in a world biased against creative ideas. The Mousetrap Myth would have us believe that the world is waiting anxiously for our original creation, our novel and useful ideas. But the truth is that most people have a hard time seeing how the novel can be useful. The world claims to want great ideas, but it rejects innovation all the time. Of all the myths of creativity, the Mousetrap Myth is perhaps

192

the most stifling to innovation because it doesn't concern generating ideas. Rather, it affects how ideas are implemented. It's not enough for an organization to have creative people; it has to develop a culture that doesn't reject great ideas. It's not enough for people to learn how to be more creative; they also need to be persistent through the rejection they might face. All of the ideas mentioned in this chapter were eventually adopted. When they were, it wasn't just because of their creativity, at least not at first. It was the persistence of their creators that moved them from idea to innovation. Likewise, it's not enough for leaders to make their teams more innovative. Leaders need to get better at counteracting their own bias and recognizing potential innovations sooner.

We don't just need more great ideas; we need to spread the great ideas we already have.

Notes

Chapter 1

1. Diodorus Siculus, *Bibliotheca Historica*, 4.7.1–2.
2. R. Keith Sawyer, *Explaining Creativity: The Science of Human Innovation* (Cambridge: Oxford University Press, 2012), 19.
3. Robert S. Albert and Mark A. Runco, "A History of Research on Creativity," in *Handbook of Creativity*, ed. Robert J. Sternberg (Cambridge: Cambridge University Press, 1998), 16–20.
4. Teresa M. Amabile, *Creativity in Context: Update to the Social Psychology of Creativity* (Boulder, CO: Westview, 1996), 35.
5. Teresa M. Amabile and others, "Assessing the Work Environment for Creativity," *Academy of Management Journal 39* (1996): 1155–1184.
6. Amabile, *Creativity in Context*.
7. *Ibid.*

Chapter 2

1. William Stukeley, *Memoirs of Sir Isaac Newton's Life* (1752).
2. Voltaire, *Lettres Philosophiques*.
3. Patricia Fara, "Catch a Falling Apple: Isaac Newton and Myths of Genius," *Endeavour 23* (1999): 167–170.
4. Mihaly Csikszentmihalyi, *Creativity: Flow and the Psychology of Discovery and Invention* (New York: HarperPerennial, 1997).
5. Scott Berkun, *Myths of Innovation* (Sebastopol, CA: O'Reilly, 2010).
6. Csikszentmihalyi, *Creativity*, 101.
7. Ellwood and others, "The Incubation Effect: Hatching a Solution?" *Creativity Research Journal 21* (2009): 6–14.
8. Benjamin Baird and others, "Inspired by Distraction: Mind Wandering Facilitates Creative Incubation," *Psychological Science 23*, no. 10 (2012), 1117–1122.
9. Norman R. F. Maier, "Reasoning in Humans: II. The Solution of a Problem and Its Appearance in Consciousness," *Journal of Comparative Psychology 12* (1931): 181–194.

10. David Owens, *Creative People Must Be Stopped: 6 Ways We Kill Innovation (Without Even Trying)* (San Francisco: Jossey-Bass, 2011).
11. Quoted in Matthew May, *The Laws of Subtraction: 6 Simple Rules for Winning in an Age of Excess* (New York: McGraw-Hill, 2012), 184.

Chapter 3

1. U.S. Department of Labor, "Fact Sheet #17D: Exemption for Professional Employees Under the Fair Labor Standards Act (FLSA)," *Wage and Hour Division* (July 2008).
2. R. Keith Sawyer, *Explaining Creativity: The Science of Human Innovation* (Cambridge: Oxford University Press, 2012).
3. *Ibid.*
4. *Ibid.*
5. *Ibid.*
6. Brian Caplan, *Selfish Reasons to Have More Kids: Why Being a Great Parent Is Less Work and More Fun Than You Think* (New York: Basic Books, 2011).
7. Marvin Reznikoff and others, "Creative Abilities in Identical and Fraternal Twins," *Behavior Genetics 3* (1973): 365–377.
8. *Ibid.*, 375.
9. Gary Hamel, *The Future of Management* (Boston: Harvard Business School Press, 2007).
10. R. Keith Sawyer, *Group Genius: The Creative Power of Collaboration* (New York: Basic Books, 2007).
11. *Ibid.*, 154.

Chapter 4

1. Malcolm Gladwell, "In the Air: Who Says Big Ideas Are Rare?" *New Yorker 84*, no. 13 (2008): 50–60.
2. *Ibid.*
3. *Ibid.*
4. Mark Twain and Albert Bigelow Paine, *Mark Twain's Letters, Vol. 1* (New York: Harper & Brothers, 1917), 731–732.
5. W. F. Ogburn and D. S. Thomas, "Are Inventions Inevitable?" *Political Science Quarterly 37* (1922): 83–98.
6. W. Brian Arthur, *The Nature of Technology: What It Is and How It Evolves* (New York: Free Press, 2009).
7. Robert Sutton, *Weird Ideas That Work: How to Build a Creative Company* (New York: Free Press, 2002).
8. John Steele Gordon, *The Business of America: Tales from the Marketplace—American Enterprise from the Settling of New England to the Breakup of AT&T* (New York: Walker, 2001), 103.
9. Robert A. Logan, *Shakespeare's Marlowe: The Influence of Christopher Marlowe on Shakespeare's Artistry* (Burlington, VT: Ashgate, 2007).
10. Julius Meier-Graefe, *Vincent van Gogh: A Biography* (Mineola, NY: Dover, 1987).

11. Kirby Ferguson, *Everything Is a Remix Part 2: Remix, Inc.*, directed by Kirby Ferguson (New York: Goodiebag, 2011), http://vimeo.com/19447662.

12. Pier Massimo Forni, *The Thinking Life: How to Thrive in the Age of Distraction* (New York: St. Martin's Press, 2011).

13. Andy Boynton, Bill Fischer, and William Bole, *The Idea Hunter: How to Find the Best Ideas and Make Them Happen* (San Francisco: Jossey-Bass, 2011).

14. Alexander Bain, *The Senses and the Intellect* (London: John Parker & Sons, 1855), 572.

15. Sarnoff Mednick, "The Associative Basis of the Creative Process," *Psychological Review 69* (1962): 220–232.

16. *Ibid.*, 224.

17. Hikaru Takeuchi and others, "White Matter Structures Associated with Creativity: Evidence from Diffusion Tensor Imaging," *NeuroImage 51* (2010): 11–18.

18. Hikaru Takeuchi and others, "Training of Working Memory Impacts Structural Connectivity," *Journal of Neuroscience 30*, no. 9 (2010): 3297–3303.

19. Robert K. Merton, *On the Shoulders of Giants: A Shandean Postscript* (Chicago: University of Chicago Press, 1993), 9.

20. *Ibid.*, 178.

21. R. Keith Sawyer, *Explaining Creativity: The Science of Human Innovation* (Cambridge: Oxford University Press, 2012).

22. Walter Isaacson, *Steve Jobs* (New York: Simon & Schuster, 2011), 178.

23. Malcolm Gladwell, "Creation Myth: Xerox PARC, Apple, and the Truth About Innovation," *New Yorker 87*, no. 13 (2011): 44–53.

24. Quoted in Warren Bennis, *Organizing Genius: The Secrets of Creative Collaboration* (New York: Basic Books, 1998), 66.

25. Kirby Ferguson, "*Embracing the Remix*," YouTube (June 2012), http://youtu.be/zd-dqUuvLk4.

Chapter 5

1. All quotations of Jay Martin are from a phone interview with the author, June 15, 2012.

2. R. Keith Sawyer, *Explaining Creativity: The Science of Human Innovation* (Cambridge: Oxford University Press, 2012).

3. Bruce Schector, *My Brain Is Open: The Mathematical Journey of Paul Erdos* (New York: Simon & Schuster, 1998), 14.

4. Jerry Grossman, "List of Publications of Paul Erdos: Update," Oakland University, https://files.oakland.edu/users/grossman/enp/pub10update.pdf (accessed June 2, 2012).

5. *Ibid.*

6. Don Tapscott and Anthony D. Williams, *Wikinomics: How Mass Collaboration Changes Everything* (New York: Portfolio, 2006).

7. *Ibid.*, 98.

8. Joshua Lerner, *Architecture of Innovation: The Economics of Creative Organizations* (Boston: Harvard Business Review Press, 2012).

9. Lenny Mendonca, interview with the author, December 19, 2012, San Francisco.

10. Jennifer Anastasoff, interview with the author, December 20, 2012, San Francisco.
11. Peters Sims, "Fuse Corps Becomes a BIG Bet, Thanks to Many Black Sheep" (September 11, 2011), http://petersims.com/2012/09/11/fuse-corps-becomes-a-big-bet-thanks-to-many-black-sheep/.
12. Noelle Galperin, interview with the author, December 17, 2012, San Francisco.
13. *Ibid.*
14. Mendonca, interview with the author.

Chapter 6

1. Arun Venugopal and Caitlyn Kim, "MacArthur Genius Grants Announced, Radio-lab Host Among Recipients," *WNYC News Blog* (September 20, 2011), http://www.wnyc.org/blogs/wnyc-news-blog/2011/sep/20/macarthur-genius-grants-announced/.
2. MacArthur Foundation, "Fellows Frequently Asked Questions," *MacArthur Foundation*, http://www.macfound.org/fellows-faq/ (accessed June 15, 2012).
3. Diane Couto, "Picking Winners: A Conversation with MacArthur Fellows Program Director Daniel J. Socolow," *Harvard Business Review 85* (2007): 121–126.
4. George E. Burch, "Of Venture Research," *American Heart Journal 92*, no. 6 (1976): 681–683.
5. Bradford C. Johnson, James M. Manyika, and Lareina A. Yee, "The Next Revolution in Interaction," *McKinsey Quarterly 4* (2005): 25–26.
6. Teresa M. Amabile, Elise D. Phillips, and Mary Ann Collins, "Creativity by Contract: Social Influences on the Creativity of Professional Artists" (paper presented at the meeting of the American Psychological Association, Toronto, Ontario, Canada, August 14–18, 1993).
7. Teresa M. Amabile, *Creativity in Context* (Boulder, CO: Westview Press, 1996), 107.
8. Edward Deci and Richard Ryan, *Intrinsic Motivation and Self-Determination in Human Behavior* (New York: Plenum, 1985).
9. Amabile, *Creativity in Context.*
10. David Burkus and Gary Oster, "Noncommissioned Work: Exploring the Influence of Structured Free Time on Creativity and Innovation," *Journal of Strategic Leadership 4*, no. 1 (2012): 48–60.
11. Rosabeth Moss Kanter, John Kao, and Fred Wiersema, *Innovation: Breakthrough Thinking at 3M, DuPont, GE, Pfizer, and Rubbermaid* (New York: HarperBusiness, 1997).
12. Daniel Pink, *Drive: The Surprising Truth About What Motivates Us* (New York: Riverhead, 2009).
13. Ben Casnocha, "Success on the Side," *The American*, April 24, 2009, http://www.american.com/archive/2009/april-2009/Success-on-the-Side/.
14. Pink, *Drive.*
15. Daniel Pink, "Reap the Rewards of Letting Your Employees Run Free," *Sunday Telegraph*, December 5, 2010, 8.

16. R. Keith Sawyer, *Group Genius: The Creative Power of Collaboration* (New York: Basic Books, 2007).
17. Robert Sutton, *Weird Ideas That Work: How to Build a Creative Company* (New York: Free Press, 2002).
18. Tina Seelig, *inGenius: A Crash Course in Creativity* (New York: HarperOne, 2012).
19. Jason Fried, "How to Spark Creativity," *Inc. 34*, no. 7 (2012): 37.
20. *Ibid.*

Chapter 7

1. Robert Friedel and Paul Israel, *Edison's Electric Light: Biography of an Invention* (New Brunswick, NJ: Rutgers University Press, 1986).
2. Andrew Hargadon, *How Breakthroughs Happen: The Surprising Truth About How Companies Innovate* (Boston: Harvard Business School Press, 2003).
3. Smithsonian Institute, "Edison's Story," *Smithsonian Lemelson Center*, http://invention.smithsonian.org/centerpieces/edison/000_story_02.asp (accessed July 7, 2012).
4. Hargadon, *How Breakthroughs Happen.*
5. *Ibid.*
6. *Ibid.*, 93.
7. William E. Wallace, "Michelangelo, CEO," *New York Times*, April 16, 1994, http://www.nytimes.com/1994/04/16/opinion/michelangelo-ceo.html.
8. Kevin Dunbar, "How Scientists Really Reason: Scientific Reasoning in Real-World Laboratories," in *Mechanisms of Insight*, ed. Robert J. Sternberg and Janet Davidson (Cambridge, MA: MIT Press, 1995), 365–395.
9. Brian Uzzi and Jarrett Spiro, "Collaboration and Creativity: The Small World Problem," *American Journal of Sociology 111* (2005): 447–504.
10. Jarrett Spiro, email interview with the author, December 2, 2012.
11. Brian Uzzi, email interview with the author, January 9, 2013.
12. Spiro, interview with the author.
13. Uzzi, interview with the author.
14. Andy Boynton, Bill Fischer, and William Bole, *The Idea Hunter: How to Find the Best Ideas and Make Them Happen* (San Francisco: Jossey-Bass, 2011).
15. All quotations of Gianfranco Zaccai are from a phone interview with the author, December 4, 2012.

Chapter 8

1. Briane Dumaine, Julie Sloane, Kemp Powers, and Julia Boorstin, "How We Got Started," *Fortune Small Business 14*, no. 7 (2004): 92–104.
2. Andy Boynton, Bill Fischer, and William Bole, *The Idea Hunter: How to Find the Best Ideas and Make Them Happen* (San Francisco: Jossey-Bass, 2011), 53.
3. David Kesmodel, "Revolutionizing American Beer," *Wall Street Journal*, April 19, 2010, http://online.wsj.com/article/SB10001424052702304510004575185931547860908.html.
4. *Ibid.*

5. Boynton, Fischer, and Bole, *The Idea Hunter*, 76.

6. Quoted in Scott Berkun, *Myths of Innovation* (Sebastopol, CA: O'Reilly 2010), 88.

7. This and later quotations of R. Keith Sawyer in this chapter are from a phone interview with the author, December 10, 2012.

8. R. Keith Sawyer, *Zig Zag: The Surprising Path to Greater Creativity* (San Francisco: Jossey-Bass, 2013) and *Explaining Creativity: The Science of Human Innovation* (Cambridge: Oxford University Press, 2012), 88–89.

9. Alex Osborn, *Applied Imagination: Principles and Procedures of Creative Problem Solving* (New York: Charles Scribner's Sons, 1957).

10. *Ibid.*, 233–242.

11. Anne K. Offner, Thomas J. Kramer, and Joel P. Winter, "The Effects of Facilitation, Recording, and Pauses on Group Brainstorming," *Small Group Research 27* (1996): 283–298.

12. Osborn, *Applied Imagination*.

13. IDEO, "*About IDEO*," IDEO, http://www.ideo.com/about/ (accessed July 13, 2012).

14. IDEO, "Our Approach: Design Thinking," IDEO, http://www.ideo.com/about/ (accessed July 13, 2012).

15. IDEO, "About IDEO," IDEO, http://www.ideo.com/about/ (accessed July 13, 2012).

16. Tina Selig, *inGenius: A Crash Course in Creativity* (New York: HarperOne, 2012).

17. Tom Kelley, *The Art of Innovation: Lessons in Creativity from IDEO, America's Leading Design Firm* (New York: Crown Business, 2001), 56.

18. *Ibid.*, 57.

19. *Ibid.*, 56.

20. Tom Kelley, "Prototyping Is the Shorthand of Design," *Design Management Journal 12* (2001): 35–42.

Chapter 9

1. Walter Isaacson, *Steve Jobs* (New York: Simon & Schuster, 2011), 431.

2. Ed Catmull, "How Pixar Fosters Collective Creativity," *Harvard Business Review 86*, no. 9 (2008): 65–72.

3. Ed Catmull, interview with Martin Giles, the Innovation Summit, March 23–24, 2010, Haas School of Business, University of California, Berkeley.

4. Quoted in Andy Boynton, Bill Fischer, and William Bole, *The Idea Hunter: How to Find the Best Ideas and Make Them Happen* (San Francisco: Jossey-Bass, 2011), 109.

5. Alex Osborn, *Applied Imagination: Principles and Procedures of Creative Problem Solving* (New York: Charles Scribner's Sons, 1957).

6. Charlan Nemeth and others, "The Liberating Role of Conflict in Group Creativity: A Study in Two Countries," *European Journal of Social Psychology 34* (2004): 365–374.

7. *Ibid.*, 372.

8. Nancy Lowry and David W. Johnson, "Effects of Controversy on Epistemic Curiosity, Achievement, and Attitudes," *Journal of Social Psychology 115* (1981): 31–43.

9. Peter Drucker, *The Effective Executive* (New York: HarperBusiness, 2006), 148.

10. Robert Sutton, *Weird Ideas That Work: 11½ Practices for Promoting, Managing, and Sustaining Innovation* (New York: Free Press, 2002), 85.

11. David Freeman, "Say Hello to Your New Brain," *Inc. 33*, no. 10 (2012): 72–78.

12. Phil Libin and Guy Kawasaki, "Creative Power," *NYSE Magazine*, http://www.nysemagazine.com/ceo-report/evernote (accessed December 12, 2012).

13. Sutton, *Weird Ideas That Work*.

14. *Ibid.*, 87.

15. Warren Bennis, *Organizing Genius: The Secrets of Creative Collaboration* (New York: Basic Books, 1998), 122.

16. Peter Sims, *Little Bets: How Breakthrough Ideas Emerge from Small Discoveries* (New York: Free Press, 2011).

17. Quoted in Sims, *Little Bets*, 71.

18. Catmull, interview with Martin Giles

Chapter 10

1. Matthew May, *The Laws of Subtraction: Six Simple Rules for Winning in the Age of Excess* (New York: McGraw-Hill, 2012), 113.

2. Larry Abramson, "How a Promise Led to Innovation: A Peanut Sheller," NPR: All Things Considered, November 10, 2010, http://www.npr.org/templates/story/story.php?storyId=130890701.

3. Tina Seelig, *inGenius: A Crash Course in Creativity* (New York: HarperOne, 2012).

4. Quoted in May, *The Laws of Subtraction*, 136.

5. Patricia Stokes, *Creativity from Constraints: The Psychology of Breakthrough* (New York: Springer, 2006), xi.

6. *Ibid.*, xii.

7. Kathleen Arnold, Kathleen B. McDermott, and Karl K. Szpunar, "Imagining the Near and Far Future: The Role of Location Familiarity," *Memory & Cognition 39* (2011): 954–967.

8. Stokes, *Creativity from Constraints*.

9. *Ibid.*

10. Kirby Ferguson, *Everything Is a Remix Part 1: The Song Remains the Same*, directed by Kirby Ferguson (New York: Goodiebag, 2011), http://vimeo.com/14912890.

11. Patricia Stokes, "Using Constraints to Generate and Sustain Novelty," *Psychology of Aesthetics, Creativity, and the Arts 1* (2007): 107–113.

12. Janina Marguc, Jens Förster, and Gerben A. Van Kleef, "Stepping Back to See the Big Picture: When Obstacles Elicit Global Processing," *Journal of Personality and Social Psychology 101*, no. 5 (2011): 883–901.

13. 37signals, "Our Story," 37signals, http://37signals.com/about (accessed July 17, 2012).

14. Jason Fried, "How I Got Good at Making Money," *Inc. 33*, no. 2 (2011): 54–60.

15. 37signals, "Our Story."

16. Jason Fried, "Starting Over," *Inc. 34*, no. 1 (2012): 40.

17. Nick Summers, "Chaos Theory," *Newsweek 155*, no. 15 (2010): 46–47.

18. Jason Fried and David Heniemeier Hansson, *Rework* (New York: Crown Business, 2011), 68.

19. *Ibid.*
20. Jason Fried, "It Takes a Village," *Inc. 34*, no. 5 (2012): 43.
21. Nick Summers, "Chaos Theory," *Newsweek 155*, no. 15 (2010): 46–47.
22. Fried and Hansson, *Rework*, 67.
23. *Ibid.*

Chapter 11

1. John H. Leinhard, "A Better Mousetrap," *Engines of Our Ingenuity*, Episode 1163, http://www.uh.edu/engines/epi1163.htm (accessed November 17, 2012).
2. Elting E. Morison, *Men, Machines, and Modern Times* (Cambridge, MA: MIT Press, 1966).
3. Quoted in Scott Berkun, *Myths of Innovation* (Sebastopol, CA: O'Reilly, 2010), 59.
4. Eric Ries, *The Lean Startup: How Today's Entrepreneurs Use Continuous Innovation to Create Radically Successful Businesses* (New York: Crown Business, 2011), 111.
5. Dave Owens, *Creative People Must Be Stopped: 6 Ways We Kill Innovation (Without Even Trying)* (San Francisco: Jossey-Bass, 2011), 126–127.
6. Tina Seelig, *inGenius: A Crash Course in Creativity* (New York: HarperOne, 2012).
7. Kevin Davies, "Public Library of Science Opens Its Doors," *Bio-IT World*, November 15, 2003, http://bio-itworld.com/archive/111403/plos/.
8. Berkun, *Myths of Innovation*, 57.
9. Rob Kaplan, *Science Says: A Collection of Quotations on the History, Meaning, and Practice of Science* (New York: Stonesong, 2003), 55.
10. Scott Kirsner, *Inventing the Movies: Hollywood's Epic Battle Between Innovation and the Status Quo, from Thomas Edison to Steve Jobs* (n.l.: CinemaTech Books, 2008), 18.
11. Plato, *Phaedrus*.
12. Jennifer S. Mueller, Shimul Melwani, and Jack A. Goncalo, "The Bias Against Creativity: Why People Desire but Reject Creative Ideas," *Psychological Science 23* (2012): 13–17.
13. David Burkus and David Owens, *LDRLB*, Episode 303, podcast audio, March 5, 2012, http://ldrlb.co/2012/03/0303-david-owens/.
14. Mueller, Melwani, and Goncalo, *"The Bias Against Creativity."*
15. Gary Hamel, *The Future of Management* (Boston: Harvard Business School Press, 2007).
16. Gregory Berns, *Iconoclast: A Neuroscientist Reveals How to Think Differently* (Boston: Harvard Business Review Press, 2010), 72.
17. *Ibid.*
18. Hamel, *Future of Management*.
19. William C. Taylor, "Here's an Idea: Let Everyone Have Ideas," *New York Times*, March 26, 2006, http://www.nytimes.com/2006/03/26/business/yourmoney/26mgmt.html?.
20. Hamel, *Future of Management*.
21. Taylor, "Here's an Idea."

Acknowledgments

The cover of this book ironically conforms to the Lone Creator Myth: there is only one name on the front. But no book is the work of solely one person. Without the collaboration and help of so many individuals, this book would not have made it into your hands:

Karen Murphy, Teresa Hennessey, John Maas, Amy Packard, Carol Hartland, Michael Friedberg, Ali de Leon, and the entire team at Jossey-Bass.

Giles Anderson, whose simple email started this whole project.

Keith Sawyer, Dan Ariely, Jarrett Spiro, Brian Uzzi, Gianfranco Zaccai, Alanna Fincke, Nate Rosenthal, and Jay Martin, who were so generous to lend their time to add color to their stories.

Jennifer Anastasoff, Lenny Mendonca, Noelle Galperin, Jeremy Goldberg, and everyone else at Fuse Corps.

Susan McCalmont and all the folks at Creative Oklahoma who were a source of constant support.

Peter Sims, Scott Berkun, Dave Owens, Matthew May, and Soren Kaplan, who from time to time tolerated my efforts to express some idea or another and gave much-needed feedback.

Jocelyn Glei and Sean Blanda at *99U*, who lent me their platform to test many of the concepts and stories in this book.

Elliot Samuel Paul, Scott Barry Kaufman, and Milena Fisher, who created an online hub for discussions about creativity.

My past professors and teachers, Dr. Gary Oster, Dr. Linda Gray, Dr. Wendy Shirk, Christine Franzeim, and Michael Mann, who taught me about innovation, how to be creative, how to write, and, thankfully, how to work.

Matt Mallino, who was always willing to download more articles and make more photocopies. Rebecca Gunn, who was always willing to proofread. And all my students at Oral Roberts University, who were the perfect group to experiment with. (Everything is a prototype.)

Dr. Steve Greene, who provided the mentorship and motivation (and constraints) needed for my own creativity to flourish, and the entire faculty at the College of Business at Oral Roberts University for their support and encouragement.

My wife, Janna, who somehow tolerates all of my ideas, even when they aren't novel or useful.

About the Author

David Burkus is assistant professor of management at the College of Business at Oral Roberts University, where he teaches courses on creativity, innovation, entrepreneurship, and organizational behavior. He is the founder and editor of *LDRLB*, an online publication that shares insights from research on leadership, innovation, and strategy.

His work on leadership, creativity, and innovation has been published in numerous scholarly journals and practitioner publications. He is also a contributing writer for *99U* and the *Creativity Post*. As a presenter, he has spoken on leadership and innovation to a diverse set of audiences, from start-ups to Fortune 500 companies to the U.S. Naval Academy.

David is a graduate of Oral Roberts University and holds a master of arts in organizational dynamics from the University of Oklahoma. He also holds a doctorate of strategic leadership from Regent University. David lives outside Tulsa, Oklahoma, with his wife and son.

For more information, please visit http://davidburkus.com.

Index

A

Abumrad, J., 88–90
Academy Awards, 147
Adjacent possible, 54–55
Adler, J., 183–184
Advanced Research Project Agency (ARPA), 63
Agreement, 152
Aiken, H. H., 182
Air technology, 120
Alternate use tests, 23
Alto, 62
Amabile, T., 6, 8, 11, 93, 94–95, 164
American Psychological Association (APA), 35–36
American Red Cross, 137
Anastasoff, J., 82
Ancient Greeks: beliefs of, about creativity, 2–3; development of myths by, 1, 2; eureka moments of, 19; muses of, 1–3
Android mobile phone, 64
Animators, 155–157
Ankle injuries, 121–122
Annus Mirabilis (Einstein), 72
Anthropology research 111–112
APA. *See* American Psychological Association
Apple, 60–65
Apple Stores, 144
Applied Imagination (Osborn), 132, 148
Archimedes, 19–20, 26, 27
Arguments, 120, 151–153
ARPA. *See* Advanced Research Project Agency

Art, 56, 160
Arthur, W. B., 53, 63
Artists, 94–95, 110
Associative thinking, 57
Athletes, 121
Atlassian, 99
AT&T, 51
Automobile paint, 96–97

B

Backpack tool, 173
Bain, A., 57
Baird, B., 24–25
Basecamp tool, 172–173
Basketball players, 121
Bass, R., 110
BBDO, 132
Beat the Dealer (book), 154
Beer industry, 126–129
Bell, A. G., 50–51, 55
BellKor's Pragmatic Chaos, 81
Bernard, E., 56
Bernard of Chartres, 60
Bias, 185–188
Big Five. *See* Five-factor model of personality
Bingham, A., 78–79
Bird, B., 146–147
Blank slates, 164–165
Bohlin, P., 144
Bookmarks, 28–30
Bootlegging policy, 99
Boredom, 165
Boston Beer Company, 128, 129
Boston Consulting Group, 126

Bow Jones, 190
Brains: components of, 58–59; mapping of, 59; size of, 35
Brainstorming: after market research, 138–139; benefits of, 126; collaboration in, 133–134; conflict and, 149–150; in creative process, 130–132; definition of, 129–130; effective methods for, 138–139, 140; examples of, 127, 136–140; improper technique for, 132; power of, 133–134; research on, 149–150; rules for, 132–133, 148; shortcomings of, 129, 135–136
Brainstorming Myth: description of, 13, 125–126; effects of, 140
Brandis, J., 161–164
Breed Myth: description of, 12, 33–34; integration of personnel and, 41–47; persuasiveness of, in organizations, 34–35, 47–48; reliance on, 47–48; studies related to, 35–41
Broadway productions, 112–117
Brown, T., 137
Budweiser, 126
Burch, G., 91
Bush, V., 63
Business school students, 82

C

Calculus, 52
Calliope, 2
Cameras, 182–183
Campbell, J., 56
Campfire chat room, 173
Canby, M., 52
Cancer treatment, 183–184
Canfield, D., 63
Capital, 174
Catmull, E., 143, 146, 156–157
Centre of the Mind, 23
CEO: decision making by, 47; selection of, 43
Change, fear of, 181
Chaucer, G., 3
Chemistry, 77–78
Children Now, 83–84
Children's Movement of California, 83–84
Christianity, 3
Civic engagement, 81–85
Class 1 and 2 disagreements, 155
Clio, 2, 3
Cognitive constraints, 168–169
Cohesive Myth: description of, 13–14, 141–142; origin of, 148–149; problems with, 157

Collaboration: in brainstorming, 133–134; conflict in, 150–155; environment for, 144–146; goal of, 120; importance of, 117; Lone Creator Myth and, 108–124; versus noncollaboration, 66; in organizational structures, 44; of outside experts, 81
Columbia University, 52, 165
Combinatorial evolution, 53–54
Commissioned artwork, 94
Compensation, financial, 95
Componential model of creativity, 6–10
Computers, filmmaking and, 142–143
Confabulation, 27
Conflict: brainstorming and, 149–150; in collaboration, 150–155; creative environments and, 142, 145–146; diversity and, 152; end products and, 151; to enhance creativity, 149–152; examples of, 153–157; personality in, 154–155; types of, 152–153, 155
Connecticut Twin Registry, 40
Constraints: benefits of, 160, 164–166; examples of, 161–166, 171–176; ill effects of, 167; need for, 160; problem solving and, 170; research on, 170–171; self-imposed, 166–167; types of, 167–170
Constraints Myth: description of, 14, 159–160; people's acceptance of, 175–176; rationality of, 164
Continual improvement, 139
Continuum, 117–124
Convergent thinking, 131
Coors, 126
Cornell University, 185
Corning, 100
Cost constraints, 161–164
Craft brewing revolution, 128
Creative environment: brainstorming and, 136; for collaboration, 144–146; conflict and, 142, 145–146; examples of, 142, 144–146; myths about, 149; people's conception of, 141
Creative industries, 34–35
Creative processes, stages of, 21–31, 130–132, 135
Creative professions, 34
Creatives: brain structure of, 59; measurement of personality of, 38; in organizational structure, 41, 42–47; stereotypes about, 36; versus suits, 34
Creativity: ancient Greek beliefs about, 2–3; conflict to enhance, 149–152; definition of, 5; as divine gift,

Index

2–4; effects of expertise on, 66–67; empirically proven model of, 5; influences on, 6; innovation's relationship to, 6–10, 15; origin of, 5, 10–11, 65; people's perception of, 186; versus repetitiveness, 93

Creativity-relevant processes: description of, 7; learning of, 9

Credit, for ideas, 66

Criticism: brainstorming and, 148, 150–151; end products and, 151–152, 155–157; plussing of, 155–157; research on, 150–151

Cross-functional work, 10

Crowdsourcing, 81

Csikszentmihalyi,M., 21–23, 28, 30, 130

Customer observation, 138

Cyberknife treatment, 184

D

Da Vinci, L., 22

Dailies, 146, 157

Dante, 3

Darwin, C., 22, 53

David (Michelangelo), 160

Davies, R., 21

DC Promise Neighborhood Initiative, 84–85

Dealer meetings, 154

Deci, E., 95

Delacroix, E., 56

Density, measure of, 19–20

Design thinking, 137–140

Diffusion tensor imaging, 59

Digital cameras, 182–183

Dimmler, E., 84

Disagreements, 151–153, 155

DISC, 38

Disney, W., 57

Disraeli, I., 19

Divergent thinking ability: in creative process, 131; research on, 59

Diversity, of thought, 79–80; conflict and, 152; innovation and, 115, 119; of inventors, 116–117; in laboratory research, 112, 116; in theater, 115, 116

Dizygotic twins, 39–40

Domain constraints, 167–168

Domain-relevant skills: description of, 6–7; importance of, 8–9. *See also* Expertise

Dorsey, J., 100

Drew, D., 96–99

Dunbar, K., 111–112, 116, 117

DuPont, 42

E

Edible Schoolyard project, 84

Edison, T., 22, 51, 106–110, 116–117

Einstein, A., 35, 71–72

Elaboration, 28

Elaboration rate, 74

Eli Lilly, 78

Elixir, 44

Emotional conflict. *See* Interpersonal conflict

Engineers, 68–70

Englebart, D., 63

Enlightenment, 3

Entrepreneurship: fears related to, 182; great idea and, 4

Epic poems, 2

Epiphanies, 17

Erato, 2

Erdos, P., 75–76, 86

Ethnographers, 138

Ethnography, 111–112

Eureka Myth: creative stages and, 21–23, 28–31; description of, 11–12, 17–18; incubation period and, 21–26; sudden inspiration and, 21–31; telling stories about, 17–20

Evaluation: apprehension about, 148; importance of, 28

Evernote, 153–154, 157

Evolutionary theory, 53, 54

Experimenting, at work, 97–103

Expert Myth: age and, 71–75; description of, 12–13, 67, 85; examples of, 68–71, 77–85; key to combating, 86; quantity versus quality and, 73–6

Expertise: age and, 71–72; effect of, on creativity, 66–67, 74–75, 76. *See also* Domain-relevant skills

Extrinsic motivation: description of, 93–94; effects of, 95; to enhance intrinsic motivation, 96

F

Facebook, 101–102

Factory work, 92

Families, genetics of, 39–41

Farming, 161–164

Fast Company magazine, 137

Feature creep, 173

Feedback, 139

Fellowships, 82–83

Filaments, 107

Finding Nemo (film), 146, 147

First chorus, 168

Five-factor model of personality (Big Five), 38
Fixed form, 160
Flash Gordon serials, 56
Floor cleaning products, 119–120
Ford, H., 55–56, 109
Fortune magazine, 137
Franklin, B., 3
Fraternal twins, 39–40
Fried, J., 102–103, 171–175
Friedel, R., 106–107
"The Frost King" (Keller), 52
Fry, A., 28–30, 99
Fulton, R., 55
Fun workplace, 13
Fuse Corps, 81–83, 85

G

Galileo, 52
Galperin, N., 83–84
Gans, L., 84–85
Gates, B., 61
General Motors, 151
Genetics: description of, 38–39; research on, 39–41
Genius, 89
Genius grants, 99
Gilmore, G., 56–57
Goldberg, J., 85
Gordon, A., 145
Gore, R., 42
Gore, W. L., 42
Gore-Tex, 42
Grafman, L., 162–164, 176
Grants, 89, 96, 99
Graphical user interface (GUI), 60–65
Gravity, force of, 18–19, 20
Gray, E., 50–51, 55
Gray matter, 58
Guilford, J. P., 35–36
Guitar strings, 43–44, 99–100
Guns, 178–181
Gutenberg, J., 55

H

Hack weeks, 100–101
Hack-a-thons, 101–102
Haiku, 160
Haiti, 162–163
Hansson, D. H., 172–175
Harmonic telegraph, 50
Harvard Business Review, 90
Health care environment, 122
Heineken beer, 127
Henry V (Shakespeare), 3

Henry VI plays (Shakespeare), 56
The Hero with a Thousand Faces (Campbell), 56
Hierarchical structure, 46
Hierarchy of no, 188
Highrise tool, 173
Historiometric method, 72–73
HMS *Scylla*, 179
HMS *Terrible*, 180
Humanities scholars, 74
Humboldt State University, 162

I

Icons, 63
Ideas, generating. *See* Brainstorming
Ideas, great: combining, 131; externalization of, 131, 134, 135; inspiration for, 4; in model of creativity, 8; new myths about, 11–15; originality of, 49–50, 52; rejection of, 182–192; sharing of, 102, 181–182; source of, 5, 10–11, 15, 20, 49; to start a business, 4; uncertainty and, 185–187
Ideation rate, 74–75
Identical twins, 39–40
IDEO, 136–140
The Iliad (epic poem), 2, 3
Ill-structured problems, 170
Imported beer, 127
"Improvement in Electric Lights" (Edison), 107
Improvisation, 134
Incentive Myth: creative work and, 93; description of, 13, 87–88; examples of people departing from, 88–92, 96–103; history of, 92; intrinsic motivation and, 103; research on, 93–95
Incentives: effective structuring of, 94–96; ill effects of, 95; purpose of, 87; structuring of, 95–96
The Incredibles (film), 147
Incubation effect, 23–24
Incubation stage: description of, 21–23, 131; function of, 23–26; prolonged, 28–30; requirements for, 31; studies of, 23–24
Industrial era, 92
Inferno (Dante), 3
InnoCentive, 78–80, 85
Innovation: creativity's relationship with, 6–10, 15; design thinking and, 137–140; diversity and, 115, 119; organizational structure and, 42–47; source of, 164
INSEAD, 112

Index

Insight stage, 22
Inspiration, sudden: stories for, 26–27; triggers for, 21–31
Institute for Personality Assessment and Research (IPAR), 37
Intellectual conflict. *See* Task conflict
Intellectual property, 12
International Design Excellence Awards, 118, 137
Interns, 70, 71
Interpersonal conflict, 152–153
Intrinsic motivation: description of, 93; enhancement of, 95–96; Incentive Myth and, 103; studies of, 94–95
Inverted-U function, 72–74
IPAR. *See* Institute for Personality Assessment and Research
iPhone, 64
The Iron Giant (film), 47
IRS, 34
Israel, P., 106–107
IV bags, 122

J

J. Walter Thompson, 165
Jehl, F., 110
Job growth, 93
Jobs, S., 61–65, 143–145
Johnson, D., 151
Johnson, K., 84
Johnson, S., 54–55, 65
Jordan, M., 120
Judgment, 181
"Just Do It" slogan, 56–57

K

Kauffman, S., 54
Keller, H., 52, 56
Kelley, T., 138, 139
King Hiero, 19
Koch, J., 126–129, 135, 136
Kodak, 182–183
Krulwich, R., 88
Kurosawa, A., 56

L

Laboratory research, 111–112
Landfills, 162–163
Lasseter, J., 143, 144
Lattice organizational structure, 43
Lauterbur, P. C., 184
Lavoie, J., 189–192
Leaders, organizational, 43
Learning, commitment to, 10
Led Zeppelin, 169

Leibniz, G., 52
Les Neufs Soeurs (Masonic lodge), 3
Libin, P., 153–154
Lichty, L., 84
Lightbulb, 106–110
Lisa computer, 62
Lone Creator Myth: current companies defying, 117–124; description of, 13, 105; effects of, 123–124; examples of, 106–110; popularity of, 105–106, 110; studies of, 111–117
Louis Koch Lager, 128
Lowry, N., 151
Lucas, G., 56, 142–143
Lucasfilm, 143
Lucky 7 Lounge, 145

M

MacArthur Fellowship, 88–92, 96, 103
MacArthur, J. D., 90–91
MacHeads, 61
Macintosh operating system, 60–65
Maier, N., 26–27
Malian Peanut Sheller, 162
Marino, J., 189–192
Market research, 137–138
Marlowe, C., 56
Martin Bionics, 68–71
Martin, J., 68–71, 76
Masking tape, 98
Mathematics, 75–76
Matrixed organization, 46
May, M., 160
McKinsey & Company, 85, 93
McKnight, W., 98–99
Media, 105–106
Mednick, S., 57–58
Memory, 58
Mendonca, L., 82, 85
Menlo Park, 107–109
Michelangelo, 22, 110, 160
Microbiologists, 111–112
Microsoft, 60–65
Miller beer, 126
Millet, J.-F., 56
Model T, 55–56
Monozygotic twins, 39–40
Motivation: importance of, 93; incentives for, 92; studies of, 94–95; types of, 93–94
Mouse, computer, 60, 61, 62, 63, 139
Mousetrap Myth: description of, 14, 177; falsehood of, 192–193; rejection and, 182–192; in the sciences, 184–185; uncertainty and bias and, 185–188

Mousetraps, 178
Moveable type, 55
Movie streaming, 81
Movie studios, 144–146
Muckers, 109–110, 116–117
Mueller, J., 185
Mueller, W., 77–78, 80
Multiples, phenomenon of, 52–55
Murder boards, 189
Muses: description of, 1–2; development of, 2; warnings about, 2–3; worship of, 2
Museums, 3–4
Musicals, 112–117
Mutual Fun system, 190–192
Myers, D., 43–44, 100
Myers-Briggs Type Indicator, 23, 24, 38
Myths: definition of, 1; development of, 1, 2; function of, 14–15; new types of, 11–15; stubborn belief in, 14–15; in Western society, 3–4

N

NASA, 42
National Public Radio, 88
Nature, versus nurture, 39–41
Naval gunnery, 178–181
Navone, V., 156–157
NBA players, 121
Necessity, 53
Nemeth, C., 149–150
Netflix, 80–81, 85
New York City, 117
New York Public Radio, 88
Newton, I., 11, 18–20, 26, 27, 52, 60
Newton, Massachusetts, 117
Nike, 56–57, 120
Nonprofit organization, 81–85
Notes, 29–30
Novels, writing, 4
Nurture, versus nature, 39–41

O

Oberlin College, 88
Observations, 138
The Odyssey (epic poem), 2, 3
Ogburn, W., 52, 53, 54
Openness to ideas, 10
Operating systems, 60–65
Oral-B Glide, 42
Organizational structure: collaboration in, 44; creatives versus suits, 41; examples of, 42–47; to integrate creatives and suits, 42–47; restructuring of, 46

Originality Myth: description of, 12, 49–50; examples of, 50–53, 54–56, 60–65; measures related to, 56–60; technology development and, 53–55; truth about, 65–66
Osborn, A., 132–133, 140, 148
Owens, D., 188

P

Painting cars, 96–97
Paintings, 56
Palo Alto Research Center (PARC), 62, 154–155
Paris, France, 117, 150
Passion. See Task motivation
Pattern-recognizing algorithms, 191
Pauling, L., 21, 129
Payroll processing, 34
Peanuts, 161–164
Personal computers, 60–65
Personality, 7; in conflicts, 154–155; measurement of, 38; new creativity myths about, 12; research on, 36–38
Pets.com, 168
Pharmaceutical companies, 77–78
Phase Zero, 118
Photocopier, 6
Physics researchers, 71–73
Pixar Animation Studios, 142–147, 155–157
Plagiarism, 52
Plastic waste, 162–163
Plato, 1–2
Playwrights, 73
Plussing, 155–157
Poetry, 2, 160
Polytetrafluoroethylene (PTFE), 42
Poncairé, H., 22–23
Porter, C., 113
Post-it Note, 28–31, 99
Practicality, 185–187
Pratt Institute, 165
Preparation, 28
Presidential addresses, 36
Pricing constraints, 174
Principles of Management classrooms, 87
Printing press, invention of, 55
Problem solving: constraints and, 170; taking a break from, 25–26; websites for, 78–80
Problems, defining, 130
Procter & Gamble, 42, 119–120
Product development, 43
Productivity, 91–92

Progress prizes, 80
Prosthetic devices, 68–71
Prototypes, 139
Psychology research, 111–112
PTFE. *See* Polytetrafluoroethylene
Pygmalion system, 63

Q

Q, 114–115
Quetelet, A., 72–73

R

Race to the Top goals, 84
Radiation therapy, 183–184
Radiolab program, 88
R&D departments, 77
Recommendation algorithm, 80
Reebok, 120–123
Remote associates test (RAT), 57–58
Repetitive work, 92, 93
Research, 137–138
Reward systems. *See* Incentives
Reznikoff, M., 40
Ribbon, 153
Ries, E., 182
Risk-averse people, 7
Risk-takers, 7
Rite-Solutions, 188–192
Robertson, J., 183
Robotics technology, 68–71
Roosevelt, T., 181

S

Sacramento Unified School District, 84
Sales, 168
Salk, J., 21
Samuel Adams Boston Lager, 128, 135,
  136
San Francisco, 117, 150
Sandpaper, 96–98
Savings Bonds, 190
Sawyer, R. K., 130–132, 133–136, 140
Science, field of: Lone Creator Myth
  in, 111–112; Mousetrap Myth in,
  184–185
Scientific method, 5
Scott, P., 179–181
Screenwriting, 110
Secrecy, 182
Seekers, 79
Selective forgetting, 25–26
Self-imposed constraints, 166–177
Semco, 45–47
Semler, A. C., 45
Semler, R., 45–47

Service projects, 81–85
Shakespeare, W., 3, 56
Sharing ideas, 102, 181–182
Shelling peanuts, 161–164
Ships, 178–181
Shoes, 120–123
Silicon Valley Talent Partnership, 85
Silver, S., 28–30, 99
Simonton, D. K., 73–74
Simplicity, 173–174, 175
Sims, P., 83
Sims, W. S., 178–181
Sistine Chapel, 110
Sketchpad system, 63
Skunky beer, 127
Sloan, A., 151–152
Slogans, 56–57
Small-world network, 114
Small-world quotient, 114–115
Smith, A. R., 143
Smithsonian, 107
Social capital, 82–83
Social environment: description of, 8;
  importance of, 10
Social scientists, 74
Socolow, D. J., 88–89, 90
Socrates, 2
Solvers, 79
Sonnets, 160
Sony, 183
Spazdaq features, 190
Spirit, 169
Spiro, J., 112–117, 123
Square, 100–101
Square Wallet, 100
"Stairway to Heaven" (Led Zeppelin),
  169
Stanford University, 152
Star Trek II: The Wrath of Kahn (film), 143
Star Wars (film), 56
Starr, J. W., 106–107
Steam engines, 55
Stereotypes, 36
Steve Jobs Building, 145
Stock markets, 189–191
Stokes, P., 165–170, 175
Stolen ideas, 51, 65, 66, 182
Stukeley, W., 18–19
Suits: brain structure of, 59; versus
  creative types, 34; in organizational
  structure, 41, 42–47
Super Bowl ads, 168
Sutherland, I., 63
Sutton, R., 152
Swiffer product line, 118, 119–120

T

Takeuchi, H., 58–59
Talent constraints, 169–170
Tamburlaine the Great (Marlowe), 56
Task conflict, 153
Task motivation: description of, 7–8;
    importance of, 9–10
"Taurus" (Spirit), 169
Tax code, 34
Taylor, B., 154–155
Taylor, F., 92, 93, 95
Teams, importance of, 117
Teflon, 42
Telegraph, 50–51, 55
Telephone, invention of, 50–51
Telescope, invention of, 52
Thamyris, 2–3
Theater, 112–117
Theologians, 3
37signals, 102–103, 171–176
This American Life (radio program), 88
Thomas, D., 52, 53, 54
Three-dimensional models, 139
3M, 28, 98–99
Tin Toy (film), 143
Tinker time programs, 96–97
Tivoli Gardens, 57
Tohoku University, 58
Top management, 10
Toy Story (film), 143–144
Traditional professions, 34
Traits. *See* Genetics; Personality
Troilus and Criseyde (Chaucer), 3
Twain, M., 52, 56
Twins, 39–41
Twitter, 100–101

U

Uncertainty, 185–188, 192
Universal Peanut Sheller, 162
University of Amsterdam, 170
University of California, Berkeley, 37,
    149
University of California, Davis, 73
University of California, Santa Barbara, 24
University of Michigan, 26

University of Minnesota, 151
University of North Carolina, 185
University of Sydney, 23
U.S. Department of Labor, 34, 47
U.S. Patent Office, 50, 51
USA Today newspaper, 168
Uzzi, B., 112–117, 123

V

Van Gogh, V., 22, 56
Variability and Creativity Lab, 165
Variability constraints, 169
Variety magazine, 113
Venture capital, 174
"Of Venture Research" (Burch), 91
Voltaire, 19

W

W. L. Gore & Associates, 41–45, 99–100
Walmart, 35
Walt Disney Company, 143
Walt Disney World, 57
Wandering mind, 24–25, 31, 50
Washington University, 130
Water displacement, 19–20
Waters, A., 84
Watson, T., 50
Webber, A. L., 113
Western Union, 51
Wharton School of Finance, 185
White matter, 58, 59, 60
Wieden, D., 56–57
Wieden+Kennedy, 56–57
Windows operating system, 60, 64
Wired magazine, 64

X

Xerox, 6, 61–62, 63

Y

Young mind phenomenon, 71–72

Z

Zaccai, G., 118–119, 120–121, 123
Zany companies, 13
Zindler, J., 120–121